EASY PORTLAND OUTDOORS

Library of Congress Control Number: 2017957324

ISBN: 9781681061313

Printed in the United States of America
18 19 20 21 22   5 4 3 2 1

Backcover: Photo courtesy Jennifer Kapnek
Front Cover: Blue Sky Rafting photo courtesy of Blue Sky Rafting
         Willamette Falls photo courtesy of Teresa Bergen
         Banks to Vernonia Trail photo courtesy of Teresa Bergen
         Cross country skiing photo courtesy of Oregon's Mount Hood
         Territory

Please note that websites, phone numbers, addresses, and company names are
subject to change or cancellation. We did our best to relay the most accurate
information available, but due to circumstances beyond our control, please do
not hold us liable for misinformation. When exploring new destinations, please do
your homework before you go.

EASY PORTLAND OUTDOORS

TERESA BERGEN

REEDY PRESS

DEDICATION

This book is dedicated to people who need
a little extra encouragement to venture out into nature.

CONTENTS

FLORA AND FAUNA

INTRODUCTION

As a child, I was artistic, not athletic. Mine was not one of those childhoods from the "good old days," when kids roamed freely over acres of land, playing in the creek and not coming inside until their moms called them for supper. Instead, I grew up on a busy street in a big city, under a flight pattern, and across the street from a naval training center. My sisters and I played inside or in our backyard. As a family, we enjoyed backcountry drives with stops at scenic vistas and overnights at the Best Western rather than backcountry treks. My street smarts developed more than my wilderness survival skills—I had more practice dodging drunken sailors than bears.

So when I moved to Portland, Oregon, as an adult, the world of people wearing GORE-TEX and driving Subaru wagons outfitted with kayak racks was a little alien. Not only did I lack a tent, but I also didn't seem to have the camping gene.

However, once I got over my initial shock at the long, gloomy season that can stretch from late fall to early summer, I noticed that the rain made everything green and beautiful. I detected a small inner urge to hike. When I met my husband, whom I term Sasquatch in a man's body, I went outside more. I got better gear and learned to befriend snow, at least for a couple of hours. I became acquainted with small, nonmotorized watercraft, such as tubes, kayaks, stand-up paddleboards, and rafts. While I'm still a bit of a chicken and more comfortable in the middle of an unknown city than in the wilderness, I'm now sort of outdoorsy. I even get excited about REI sales.

I share this history because I'm sure there are other people like me, who faintly hear the call of the wild. Maybe you think of yourself as a city person. Or perhaps age, injury, or the presence of young children has rendered outdoor adventures less accessible than they once were. This book is about going outside and breathing some fresh air while exercising, absorbing culture, or maybe just getting something to eat. Adventures range from no skills required to minimal skills or at least the willingness to try. Some activities are free. Others cost a little or a lot, depending on the scope of the adventure.

Easy Portland Outdoors is divided into five loosely defined sections—activities focusing on water, land, flora and fauna, history/food/culture, and fun and games. You'll find answers to questions about whether you can bring your dog, kids, or wheelchair on each adventure, the best time of year to go, and special equipment you'll need. Note that all distances are from Pioneer Courthouse Square at the center of downtown Portland.

I hope this book inspires you to go outside and try something new. I know it's not always comfortable to expand one's horizons, but whether my husband was laughing at my "granny swing" as I wielded a golf club for the first time, or I was praying not to fall off a raft and into the rapids, or a small ruminant was chewing my hair during goat yoga, I had a lot of fun writing this book.

ACKNOWLEDGMENTS

Thanks to all the folks who aided me in and accompanied me on these adventures, including: Alder Creek Kayak, Canoe, Raft & SUP, Ross Beach, Joanne Bergen, Blue Sky Rafting, Crystal Springs Rhododendron Garden, Alfie Davis, Heide Davis, Julia Demorest, Michael Detlef, Envi Adventures, Goat Yoga, Hawthorne Ghost Tour, Jennifer Kapnek, Lan Su Garden, Thomas Dietzel, Annabelle Mallory, ClaireMarie Mallory, Lainey Morse, Christina Moss, Mount Hood Adventure, Mount Hood Skibowl, Next Adventure, Rodney Noland, Oregon Coast Railriders, Oregon Garden Resort, Oregon's Mt. Hood Territory, Oregon Zoo, Gideon Parque, Portland Japanese Garden, Portland Highland Games, Portland Walking Tours, Darin Puntillo, Rudy the keeshond, Casey Seyb, Travel Portland, UnCruise Adventures, Visit Salem, Visit Vancouver USA, Vancouver Segway Tours, Willamette Jetboat Excursions and Yoga to You. And thanks to everyone at Reedy Press for making this book look so good.

Special thanks to my family for their support, love and encouragement: my parents, F. Newman and Dee, my sisters Joanne and Margo and my cousin Julia. And especially my husband Gideon and keeshond Rudy who get me outside a lot more, and patiently serve as models for my outdoor photos.

ON THE THE WATER

1 TAKE A KAYAKING LESSON

Give somebody a kayak and a paddle and that person will probably make it down a river eventually. But taking a lesson can turn a timid newbie into a confident paddler. Instructors at Alder Creek Kayak guide beginners into Tomahawk Bay, a sheltered part of the mighty Columbia River chosen more for calmness than scenic beauty. There you'll learn to efficiently paddle forward, backward, and even sideways. The magic of kayaking is that you sit so low in the water that it feels like being one with the river. You might find yourself eye to eye with a great blue heron standing silently on the bank or startling one into a squawking departure, wings almost grazing your head. Once the instructor deems the students competent, he ups the excitement: paddling over logs, playing kayak tag, and practicing a deep-water wet exit (a.k.a. falling out of your kayak) and then rescuing your classmates. Learning kayaking skills in this supportive environment might mark the beginning of a new outdoor passion.

200 NE Tomahawk Island Dr.,
503-285-0464   aldercreek.com
(additional stores in Tualatin, Ridgefield, and Lake Oswego)

WHEN TO GO: Year-round, but warmer months are more pleasant.

HOURS: Varies; Jantzen Beach shop is open 9:00 a.m. to 6:00 p.m.

KID-FRIENDLY: Yes, ten and up

DOG-FRIENDLY: No

WHEELCHAIR ACCESSIBLE: No

EQUIPMENT NEEDED: Quick-drying clothes, water shoes, hat, sunscreen

COST: $69 for a basic skills kayak class

ACCESSIBLE BY PUBLIC TRANSPORTATION: Yes

DISTANCE FROM DOWNTOWN PORTLAND: Eight miles

FACILITIES: Restroom, changing room, gear shop

SPECIAL COMMENTS: Borrow a wetsuit during cooler months.

2 FLOAT DOWN THE WILLAMETTE RIVER

Promoters describe the Big Float as a chance to "give our river a hug." The Willamette, that mighty river that divides Portland's east and west sides, needs one. Because the river has long been scorned for sewage overflows and being part of the Portland Harbor Superfund Site, Portlanders often want to keep a boat between themselves and the river. The Human Access Project encourages people to jump right in—with a float and a life vest—for an enormous, colorful annual beach party. Three thousand people show up to float between the Marquam and Hawthorne bridges on a flotilla of inflatable unicorns, parrots, and doughnuts, and then lounge in the water listening to bands play on a floating stage. The float route is roped off from the path of bigger ships, with volunteers in kayaks patrolling the perimeter keeping things safe for Portland's biggest pool party. Funds raised benefit the Human Access Project, which is improving the river's reputation and making it more accessible for recreational use.

707 SW Washington St., Suite 1500   thebigfloat.com

WHEN TO GO: One Saturday in July

HOURS: Afternoon

KID-FRIENDLY: Yes

DOG-FRIENDLY: A few salty dogs participate.

WHEELCHAIR ACCESSIBLE: No

EQUIPMENT NEEDED: Float vessel, life jacket

COST: $5

ACCESSIBLE BY PUBLIC TRANSPORTATION: Yes

DISTANCE FROM DOWNTOWN PORTLAND: Downtown

FACILITIES: Porta-potties, food booths, entertainment

SPECIAL COMMENTS: A paddle is very helpful; two cheap Frisbees will do in a pinch.

3 | TAKE THE POLAR PLUNGE

Some things are easier to do when about three thousand other folks around the state are doing it too, such as running into the frigid Columbia River in February and diving under. That these brave plungers are raising money for Special Olympics athletes also helps motivate them. Every winter, polar plunges take place in rivers around Oregon. Typically, about three thousand people participate, raising about $500,000 for Special Olympics. In Portland, the action happens at Broughton Beach on the Columbia. Participants who take the plunge reap rewards—a long-sleeved T-shirt and a bowl of soup. The plunge attracts the most macho philanthropists, such as teams of law enforcement officers. Anyone can sign up to participate in the 5K that precedes the plunge, the plunge itself, or the winter beach party. Those who don't even want to stick their toes in the river can pledge a donation to a plunger or just stand on the shore and cheer on those hardy souls.

5901 SW Macadam Ave., Ste. 200
503-248-0600   lungeoregon.com

WHEN TO GO: February

HOURS: Morning

KID-FRIENDLY: Yes

DOG-FRIENDLY: No

WHEELCHAIR ACCESSIBLE: No

EQUIPMENT NEEDED: A brave heart; costumes encouraged

COST: Raise at least $50 to plunge

ACCESSIBLE BY PUBLIC TRANSPORTATION: Yes

DISTANCE FROM DOWNTOWN PORTLAND: Ten miles

FACILITIES: Porta-potty, snacks

SPECIAL COMMENTS: It's scary, but you'll be a hero.

4 RAFT THE CLACKAMAS RIVER

An hour southeast of Portland, the Clackamas River roars through the Mount Hood National Forest. Several rafting outfitters offer exciting whitewater trips through intermediate class-three rapids in spring and summer. The water is higher and much wilder during spring runoff, but summer rafters find plenty of fun and wet thrills running rapids with such names as Hole in the Wall, Toilet Bowl, and Rock and Roll. After a safety talk and basic instructions, paddlers launch their rafts and attempt to stay onboard and keep paddling regardless of the raging water. Blue Sky's half-day, six-mile trip follows a classic pattern of rapids, calm pools, and then more rapids. During tranquil periods, rafters can admire old-growth forests of Douglas fir, spruce, aspen, and red cedar and delight in the antics of mergansers—mohawked ducks that masterfully navigate rapids. The lively guides joke, tell stories, and encourage groups to play rafting games that ensure maximum saturation, such as driving the raft upstream and "surfing" a rapid.

503-630-3163   blueskyrafting.com

WHEN TO GO: Hot summer days

HOURS: Half-day trips run 9:30 a.m. to 12:30 p.m. and 1:30 p.m. to 4:30 p.m. Full-day trips, 10:00 a.m. to 3:30 p.m.

KID-FRIENDLY: Minimum age is six

DOG-FRIENDLY: No

WHEELCHAIR ACCESSIBLE: No

EQUIPMENT NEEDED: Water shoes, quick-dry clothes, sunscreen, sunglasses, hat

COST: $52 for half day, $87 for full day

ACCESSIBLE BY PUBLIC TRANSPORTATION: No

DISTANCE FROM DOWNTOWN PORTLAND: Forty-two miles

FACILITIES: Restroom at put-in spot

SPECIAL COMMENTS: Blue Sky provides splash jackets, but you'll still get very wet.

5 CRUISE ON THE *PORTLAND SPIRIT*

The *Portland Spirit* family of sightseeing cruises provides the easiest way to experience local rivers. The *Portland Spirit* itself boards downtown and then plies the Willamette, offering sightseeing, dinner, lunch and brunch, and dance cruises. It even serves a Thanksgiving buffet, for passengers who'd rather cruise than cook and a holiday Cinnamon Bear cruise for children. The *Columbia Gorge Sternwheeler*, the *Spirit's* sister ship, docks at Cascade Locks in the Gorge. It has sightseeing and brunch and dinner cruises on the Columbia River. Both the *Spirit* and the *Sternwheeler* have enclosed, climate-controlled decks, or passengers can climb to the upper deck to feel the wind on their faces. These ships provide an excellent way for people who want to relax rather than row and for those with mobility impairments to be able to admire Portland's bridges and skyline. For a wilder ride, the *Portland Spirit's* thirty-five-passenger, covered jet boat *Explorer* takes passengers 120 miles round-trip on the Willamette and Columbia, stopping for lunch in Cascade Locks.

110 SE Caruthers St.
503-224-3900
portlandspirit.com

WHEN TO GO: Year-round

HOURS: Varies

KID-FRIENDLY: Yes, especially the sightseeing cruise; dinner, less so

DOG-FRIENDLY: No

WHEELCHAIR ACCESSIBLE: *Portland Spirit* and *Columbia Gorge Sternwheeler*, yes; *Explorer*, no

EQUIPMENT NEEDED: Windbreaker, hat

COST: Cruises range from $30 for sightseeing and $74 for dinner on the *Spirit* to $94 for a full day of sightseeing on the *Sternwheeler*.

ACCESSIBLE BY PUBLIC TRANSPORTATION: *Spirit* and *Explorer*, yes; *Sternwheeler*, no

DISTANCE FROM DOWNTOWN PORTLAND: *Spirit* docks downtown at Waterfront Park

FACILITIES: Restrooms, food

SPECIAL COMMENTS: Dressing up for dinner is nice, but don't wear high heels on a boat.

6 PLAY IN A FOUNTAIN

Portland is known for its rain, but summer heat waves drive temperatures into the 90s and occasionally triple digits. On these hottest days, nothing feels as good as playing in a fountain. A few of Portland's best fountains include Salmon Street Springs at Waterfront Park, with ever-changing, high-powered jets controlled by an underground computer; Jamison Square in the Pearl District, with a wading pool suitable for toddlers; and the Ira Keller Fountain downtown, which looks like a series of angular pools and waterfalls. About a dozen parks also feature splash pads, which are like an amped-up version of running through a sprinkler. In Peninsula Park, a giant green frog squirts water on kids. At Blue Lake Regional Park, plastic buckets continually fill up until they get heavy enough to dump on your head. Columbia Park has giant flower-shaped fountains. Portland's fountains and splash pads offer enough variety to entertain water-loving children all summer long. For free!

Portland Parks' list of splash pads:
portlandoregon.gov/parks/article/454927

WHEN TO GO: Summer

HOURS: The city turns splash pads on from 11:00 a.m. to 9:00 p.m. in summer.

KID-FRIENDLY: Yes

DOG-FRIENDLY: Varies

WHEELCHAIR ACCESSIBLE: Varies

EQUIPMENT NEEDED: Swimsuit, towel, sunscreen

COST: Free

ACCESSIBLE BY PUBLIC TRANSPORTATION: Yes

DISTANCE FROM DOWNTOWN PORTLAND: Varies

FACILITIES: Most parks have restrooms, but fountains don't.

SPECIAL COMMENTS: Splash pad water is for playing, not drinking.

SWIM AT POET'S BEACH

It's not Malibu or Waikiki, but Portland's new little beach under the Marquam Bridge offers seasonal swimming access to the Willamette River right downtown. The Human Access Project worked with other nonprofits and governmental bodies to remove rocks and make a small length of shoreline into a welcoming river beach. The catch? Attracting swimmers. Before a major project in 2011, the Willamette suffered from bad water and a bad reputation because of sewer runoff, but the water is cleaner now, and the cordoned-off area at Poet's Beach is clear and shallow and only two feet deep. Summer 2017 was the first season that the city employed a lifeguard every day, upping the safety quotient for those ready to trust the river. Smooth stones line the path down from the South Waterfront promenade to the beach, many engraved with Chinook words and children's poems about the river. One poem, by a fifth grader named Mikaela, sums up the whole Poet's Beach project: "Never slam it, our river Willamette."

South Waterfront Park
portlandoregon.gov/parks/73880

WHEN TO GO: Summer

HOURS: Lifeguard on duty 11:00 a.m. to 7:00 p.m.

KID-FRIENDLY: Yes

DOG-FRIENDLY: Yes

WHEELCHAIR ACCESSIBLE: No

EQUIPMENT NEEDED: Water shoes, swimwear

COST: Free

ACCESSIBLE BY PUBLIC TRANSPORTATION: Yes

DISTANCE FROM DOWNTOWN PORTLAND: One mile

FACILITIES: Picnic tables, trash cans, Porta-potty, bike racks, life jacket borrowing station

SPECIAL COMMENTS: If you're worried about water quality, consult the Portland Bureau of Environmental Services website before swimming. It tests the water weekly.

8 RENT A PEDAL BOAT AND SWIM AT BLUE LAKE REGIONAL PARK

Most tiny watercraft are powered by oars, but at Blue Lake Regional Park lake lovers can rent pedal-powered boats. On a floating bicycle built for two, visitors cruise around the lake, checking out the lotus patches, kids splashing in the swimming area, and the surrounding houses, many of which feature water slides right into the lake. The boats are easy to steer with a hand lever. Blue Lake is heaven in summer for families with water-loving kids. The spray pad features fountains and water-squirting toys that keep kids drenched and squealing with delight. Child-friendly displays in the Discovery Garden encourage touching, smelling, and digging. Children five and up can play in a shallow swim area, which is cordoned off from the rest of the lake. Basketball hoops, playing fields, and a disc golf course round out the entertainment. On a hot, clear summer day, this is a fantastic family spot to swim and picnic with a view of snow-topped Mount Hood.

21224 NE Blue Lake Rd.
oregonmetro.gov/parks/blue-lake-regional-park

WHEN TO GO: Summer for the most lake fun

HOURS: 8:00 a.m. to sunset

KID-FRIENDLY: Very

DOG-FRIENDLY: No dogs allowed

WHEELCHAIR ACCESSIBLE: Yes

EQUIPMENT NEEDED: Sunscreen, swimwear, snacks

COST: $5 for parking, $10/hour for pedal boats

ACCESSIBLE BY PUBLIC TRANSPORTATION: No

DISTANCE FROM DOWNTOWN PORTLAND: Fifteen miles

FACILITIES: Restrooms, picnic tables

SPECIAL COMMENTS: If you're renting a pedal boat solo, you can ask for an oar for easier steering.

9 SOAK IN BAGBY HOT SPRINGS

Between its natural setting, flimsily partitioned bathing kiosks, and swimsuit-optional policy, Bagby attracts wellness buffs you might not encounter in a sleek, modern spa. To get there, you hike an easy 1.5 miles through the Mount Hood National Forest. Step carefully, as you might come across newts on this moist trail. The hot springs are piped into hollowed-out logs in private bathing rooms. Buckets are provided for adding cold water so that bathers don't turn into soup. This funky attraction in a beautiful natural setting is well worth visiting, but come with a patient mind-set and be prepared for mild anarchy. Nobody is in charge, and some bathers like to wallow in their logs for hours regardless of the growing line of people waiting. Bathers who don't mind sharing can venture into the two communal tubs. If you want to be sure to have first crack at a log, you can camp a quarter mile past the springs at Shower Creek Campground and bathe at dawn.

FSR 70, Clackamas County
503-630-6861
fs.usda.gov/detail/mthood/recreation/?cid=fsbdev3_053501

WHEN TO GO: Year-round, depending on weather

HOURS: Twenty-four hours

KID-FRIENDLY: Yes, if parents are open-minded about nudity

DOG-FRIENDLY: Yes

WHEELCHAIR ACCESSIBLE: No

EQUIPMENT NEEDED: Towels, swimsuit optional

COST: $5 for the parking permit

ACCESSIBLE BY PUBLIC TRANSPORTATION: No

DISTANCE FROM DOWNTOWN PORTLAND: Sixty-seven miles

FACILITIES: Restrooms

SPECIAL COMMENTS: The road to Bagby isn't maintained during winter, so check on conditions before you make the drive.

10 EXPERIENCE THE WATERS OF BELKNAP HOT SPRINGS

A popular overnight trip from Portland, Belknap is a historic hot springs on the McKenzie River. Ever since the 1870s people have come to soak in mineral-filled water that flows out of the earth at more than 185 degrees. Visitors can pay for an hour's bathing time, buy a day pass, or stay overnight in a lodge, cabins, RV, or campsite. Water is directed into two mineral pools, basically swimming pools full of hot, steamy water loaded with lithium, sodium, calcium, potassium and a dozen other minerals. The lower pool has a gorgeous setting overlooking the fast-flowing McKenzie River and, in late summer, is bordered by enormous sunflowers. Belknap's grounds include forest trails and a secret garden full of fountains, flowers, and stone pillars inside a moss-covered stone wall. If you make the overnight trip to Belknap, allow time to walk a segment of the twenty-six-mile McKenzie River Trail. Highlights include the shockingly blue Tamolitch Pool, where a volcano-buried part of the river seeps out through porous lava, and the pounding waters of Sahalie and Koosah falls.

59296 N Belknap Springs Rd.
McKenzie Bridge
541-822-3512
belknaphotsprings.com

WHEN TO GO: Year-round

HOURS: 9:00 a.m. to 9:00 p.m. Pools are open until 10:00 p.m. for overnight guests.

KID-FRIENDLY: Yes, two and up

DOG-FRIENDLY: Dogs are not allowed at the hot springs pool but are welcome on the grounds.

WHEELCHAIR ACCESSIBLE: No

EQUIPMENT NEEDED: Bathing suit required—not a hippie hot spring

COST: $8 for one hour, $15 for a day pass. Lodging ranges from $30 for a tent site to $325 for a cabin that sleeps ten, with many options in between. All include use of hot springs.

ACCESSIBLE BY PUBLIC TRANSPORTATION: No

DISTANCE FROM DOWNTOWN PORTLAND: 164 miles

FACILITIES: Restrooms, showers, a small store with snacks and souvenirs, lodging

SPECIAL COMMENTS: Kind of far, but worth the drive

11 LEARN STAND-UP PADDLEBOARDING BASICS

Stand-up paddleboarding is a fast-growing sport that's spread over the lakes and rivers of the Northwest for the past ten years. A whole different way to enjoy the water, SUP requires more balance than kayaking but a lot less than surfing. The height advantage also allows paddleboarders to see farther than kayakers. When your legs get tired, you can kneel or even lie down on your board and watch the clouds. Alder Creek Kayak and Canoe offers an excellent three-hour beginning lesson at both its Jantzen Beach and Tryon Cove locations. At Tryon Cove, students paddle on the Willamette River at Lake Oswego. Lessons start onshore with SUP anatomy and then take to the river, where students learn basic strokes kneeling on the board before eventually standing up. By the end of three hours, students will be in the middle of the choppy river under the watchful eye of their experienced paddleboard teacher, improving their balance while looking for fish, sea lions, and adorable ducklings.

14110 Stampher Rd., Lake Oswego
971-313-4781
aldercreek.com

WHEN TO GO: When the weather is calm

HOURS: Varies

KID-FRIENDLY: Yes

DOG-FRIENDLY: No

WHEELCHAIR ACCESSIBLE: No

EQUIPMENT NEEDED: Board, personal flotation device, wetsuits (except in summer)

ACCESSIBLE BY PUBLIC TRANSPORTATION: Yes

DISTANCE FROM DOWNTOWN PORTLAND: Nine miles

FACILITIES: Porta-potty

SPECIAL COMMENTS: You might not fall in, but dress like you expect to.

12 TRY SUP YOGA

Paddleboards aren't just for paddling. People also treat them like oversized yoga mats. Several businesses in town offer SUP yoga classes. Next Adventure's relatively affordable class meets weekly during the summer at Sellwood Riverfront Park and welcomes participants with or without experience in either yoga or SUP. Students grab a board and paddle a short distance on their knees to the floating studio. Carabiners secure boards to knots on a rope so that nobody floats downriver. Thus anchored, the teacher slowly leads students through a series of seated, kneeling, and standing positions. Experienced yogis will find that the paddleboard lends a whole new element to balancing in even simple poses, and the sights, smells, sounds, and feel of the river provide a new perspective on a very old practice. Given the challenges of balancing on a floating board, traditional poses are modified, at least for beginners. At the end of class, students spend a few minutes relaxing on their backs, wavelets lapping their boards, letting go of all effort.

503-233-0706
nextadventure.net/portland-kayak-school-stand-up-paddleboard-yoga-beginner

WHEN TO GO: Summer

HOURS: Varies

KID-FRIENDLY: No

DOG-FRIENDLY: No

WHEELCHAIR ACCESSIBLE: No

EQUIPMENT NEEDED: Flip flops or water shoes

COST: $35 for Next Adventure's class; other companies vary

ACCESSIBLE BY PUBLIC TRANSPORTATION: Yes

DISTANCE FROM DOWNTOWN PORTLAND: Five miles

FACILITIES: Restroom

SPECIAL COMMENTS: This might sound intimidating, but it's really fun.

13 GO KAYAKING AT SUNSET

Because Portland skies are so often gray, Portlanders appreciate a good sunset. So Portland Kayak Company often sells out its summer sunset tours. Paddlers meet up on a South Waterfront dock, where guides tuck everybody into life jackets and demonstrate a basic paddle stroke. Then the group of up to sixteen pushes off into the gentle Willamette River. Paddlers head downriver in the main shipping channel, bobbing over the occasional wakes of speedboats. The kayakers bunch up to cross the river en masse and then hug the shore of uninhabited Ross Island. At the far end of the island, participants get a close-up look at a floating home community, including a houseboat made famous on the TV show *My Floating Home*. One guide leads, while the other brings up the rear, watching over any stragglers. The group returns on the quiet east side of Ross Island, passing a decades-old blue heron rookery and watching the fiery orb descend through the silhouettes of the island's trees and blackberry brambles.

6600 SW Macadam Ave.
503-459-4050   portlandkayak.com

WHEN TO GO: May through September

HOURS: 6:00 p.m. to 8:30ish

KID-FRIENDLY: Seven and up

DOG-FRIENDLY: No

WHEELCHAIR ACCESSIBLE: No

EQUIPMENT NEEDED: Drybag for anything you want to keep dry, sunglasses

COST: $49

ACCESSIBLE BY PUBLIC TRANSPORTATION: Yes

DISTANCE FROM DOWNTOWN PORTLAND: One mile

FACILITIES: Restroom on dock, room to lock up your possessions

SPECIAL COMMENTS: While no experience is necessary, expect a fair amount of paddling to get around the island.

14 EXPLORE A WATERFALL

Waterfalls dot the Columbia Gorge, drawing hikers who gawk and photograph and occasionally splash and shower in them. Some 2.5 million people visit Multnomah Falls annually, making it Oregon's most popular waterfall. At 620 feet, it's also one of the world's tallest. A 0.2 mile paved trail leads to a historic bridge between the falls' upper and lower cataracts. On summer weekends, this bridge is jammed with people taking selfies and group photos. Traffic thins for hardier hikers who continue up a dirt trail, making the 2.4-mile round-trip journey to the top of the falls. Most people content themselves with walking to the bridge and then poking around Multnomah Lodge. Built in 1925 out of Oregon stone, the lodge features a restaurant, gift shop, and visitors center, with exhibits on gorge geology and history. The sugary smells of soft serve and fudge permeate the area, and many visitors soon have a cone in hand. Shorter but less crowded nearby waterfalls include Latourell, Wahclella, and Lower Punchbowl.

53000 E Historic Columbia River Hwy., Bridal Veil
503-695-2376   multnomahfallslodge.com

WHEN TO GO: Year-round. In summer, weekdays are less crowded.

HOURS: The lodge is open 8:00 a.m. to 9:00 p.m.; visitors center is staffed 9:00 a.m. to 5:00 p.m.

KID-FRIENDLY: Yes

DOG-FRIENDLY: Yes

WHEELCHAIR ACCESSIBLE: Yes

EQUIPMENT NEEDED: Camera

COST: Free

ACCESSIBLE BY PUBLIC TRANSPORTATION: Yes

DISTANCE FROM DOWNTOWN PORTLAND: Thirty miles

FACILITIES: Restaurant, restroom, gift shop, visitors center

SPECIAL COMMENTS: Traffic and parking can be a beast. Consider taking the Columbia Gorge Express from Portland.

15 SWIM IN AN OUTDOOR POOL

Many Portland swimmers look forward to the opening of the city's seven public outdoor pools every summer. Each pool has a different personality, attracting its own clientele. The oval-shaped pool in Sellwood starts at zero feet deep in the shallow end, so it is better for kids than adult lap swimmers. In Southwest Portland, the Wilson pool is the city's most deluxe, with a water slide, separate lap swimming and kids' pools, a frog slide for toddlers, and a lazy river feature. Creston Park's pool, set in a cute, grassy park, lends itself to sunbathing. Because the outdoor pools are only open in the summer, they attract hordes of children. These are fun places for an inexpensive family outing. Even serious lap swimmers may brave the racket and crowds for the chance to feel the sun on their skin after three seasons of being cooped up in indoor pools.

portlandoregon.gov/parks/38284

WHEN TO GO: June to August

HOURS: Varies by pool

KID-FRIENDLY: Yes

DOG-FRIENDLY: No

WHEELCHAIR ACCESSIBLE: Grant, Sellwood, and Wilson

EQUIPMENT NEEDED: Swimsuit, towel, lock

COST: Most cost $4.25 for adults, $3.25 for children. Wilson costs $5.50 for adults, $4.50 for children.

ACCESSIBLE BY PUBLIC TRANSPORTATION: Yes

DISTANCE FROM DOWNTOWN PORTLAND: Varies

FACILITIES: Varies; most pools have locker rooms.

SPECIAL COMMENTS: Frequent swimmers can save money by buying a seasonal pass.

16 CAREEN DOWN THE RIVER ON A WILLAMETTE JETBOAT

"Only the first nine rows get wet," the captain says as passengers board the *Peregrine Falcon*, which means there's not a dry seat on these nine-row vessels. This is the journey for those who want to careen down the Willamette at fifty miles per hour, weaving between bridge pilings and doing 360s. Sudden stops send great passenger-drenching waves of water over the entire boat. The captain intersperses these wet hijinks with a history of Portland's many bridges, corny jokes, and pointing out osprey nests. He might slow down to explain Portland's importance as a grain port while motoring close to an enormous foreign ship loading up at the grain silos. The company offers one-, two-, and three-hour options. The shortest trip stays downtown, while the two-hour journey blasts all the way down to Willamette Falls in Oregon City. The longest ride takes passengers up to the Columbia and includes lunch at a floating restaurant. Even longtime Portland residents might find themselves flying down a stretch of river they've never seen.

1945 SE Water Ave.
503-231-1532
willamettejet.com

WHEN TO GO: May through October 1

HOURS: Various departures between 10:45 a.m. and 4:30 p.m.

KID-FRIENDLY: Yes

DOG-FRIENDLY: No

WHEELCHAIR ACCESSIBLE: No

EQUIPMENT NEEDED: Rain jacket, drybag if you must bring something that can't get wet

COST: The two-hour tour costs $44 for adults, $30 for children eleven and under

ACCESSIBLE BY PUBLIC TRANSPORTATION: Yes

DISTANCE FROM DOWNTOWN PORTLAND: One mile

FACILITIES: Water for sale on dock

SPECIAL COMMENTS: Not for the frail, pregnant, or people with back and neck injuries. Even on a sunny day, the water and wind combo can be very cold, so consider bringing a rain jacket.

17 GO TO THE BEACH AT SAUVIE ISLAND

During summer, beachgoers clog Highway 26 to the Oregon coast, but those who appreciate a river beach can find a sandy shore on Sauvie Island, which is much closer to home. People spread their towels over a handful of public beaches that dot the island's north and northeast coast. It feels a bit like an ocean beach. The Columbia River is tidal and large enough to produce small waves. Folks float in the water or lounge on the sand, watching large ships passing between Portland and the Pacific Ocean. At Walton Beach, one of the island's most popular and easily accessible, a sign demarcates where Walton ends and clothing-optional Collins Beach begins. Expect naked sunbathers and boaters, and beware of pleas for help with sunscreen application. People who favor more secluded beaches will enjoy Warrior Point Beach, which requires a boat or a 3.5-mile hike to reach. These beaches can be scorching at noon in August but are especially pleasant on summer evenings as the sun sets.

sauvieisland.org/visitor-information/natural-attractions/public-beaches

WHEN TO GO: Summer and other warm days

HOURS: Dawn to 10:00 p.m.

KID-FRIENDLY: Yes

DOG-FRIENDLY: Yes, but must be leashed

WHEELCHAIR ACCESSIBLE: No

EQUIPMENT NEEDED: Towels, sunscreen

COST: $10 for island parking permit

ACCESSIBLE BY PUBLIC TRANSPORTATION: No

DISTANCE FROM DOWNTOWN PORTLAND: Twenty miles

FACILITIES: Porta-potty

SPECIAL COMMENTS: These beaches are isolated, so bring plenty of water and snacks.

18 SEE WILLAMETTE FALLS BY KAYAK

By water volume, Oregon City's Willamette Falls is second only to the much better known Niagara, and it's a first in hydropower: In 1889, the Willamette Falls Electric Company transmitted electricity fourteen miles upriver to Portland. A ninety-minute guided trip led by eNRG Kayaking combines history, industry, river engineering, and wildlife viewing. Guides give paddlers an up- close view of the locks and falls. Many Portlanders have only seen the old Blue Heron paper mill from OR-99. From the river, the crumbling, deserted building towers overhead, and paddlers feel the water power that ran a sawmill here even before electricity. In spring, when the river is high, salmon and huge sturgeon jump out of the river, and barking sea lions may torpedo between a group's kayaks, hunting for dinner. Unseen, eel-like lampreys climb the waterfall with their mouths to spawn in the Willamette. Being right down there in the water with industry and wildlife is a totally different experience from viewing it from the riverbank.

1701 Clackamette Dr.
503-772-1122   enrgkayaking.com

WHEN TO GO: Spring to fall, depending on river levels

HOURS: Varies by season

KID-FRIENDLY: Yes, must be eight or older to operate a kayak.

DOG-FRIENDLY: No

WHEELCHAIR ACCESSIBLE: No

EQUIPMENT NEEDED: Hat, sunscreen, quick-dry clothes, water shoes

COST: $60 per person

ACCESSIBLE BY PUBLIC TRANSPORTATION: Yes

DISTANCE FROM DOWNTOWN PORTLAND: Fourteen miles

FACILITIES: Restroom

SPECIAL COMMENTS: Tandem kayaks are also available, but the guide didn't recommend "divorce boats" for couples.

19 TAKE A LUXURY CRUISE WITH UNCRUISE ADVENTURES

For a big adventure, board UnCruise's *SS Legacy* in Portland to explore the Columbia and Snake rivers. The Columbia River Gorge is one of Earth's most beautiful places, with the deep-blue Columbia River contrasting with the four-thousand-foot basalt cliffs carved by the ancient Missoula Flood. From Portland to the Dalles, the gorge is wooded. East of the Dalles, passengers enter an other-worldly landscape of bare, golden hills. Depending on the voyage, itineraries focus on wineries, history, or outdoor activities, including stops at museums, rafting the Deschutes River, and a jet boat ride through Hells Canyon. A fully-costumed Nez Perce storyteller might join guests aboard, or UnCruise guides might lead a rousing Pacific Northwest history-based trivia game.

Guests on this eighty-eight-passenger ship can expect evening presentations on geology, Lewis and Clark—who followed this same waterway—and Native American culture. A fully-costumed Nez Perce storyteller might join guests aboard, or UnCruise guides might lead a rousing Pacific Northwest history-based trivia game. The cruise appeals to people more interested in how ships transit locks than in the glitzier amenities of larger cruise lines. Dress is always casual, and it's perfectly all right to wear fleece to the delicious yet informal meals. For river lovers who want time to savor one of the country's most powerful rivers, a week on an UnCruise adventure will be a lifelong highlight.

888-862-8881
uncruise.com

WHEN TO GO: Late summer, fall

HOURS: Cruises run one week, from Saturday to Saturday.

KID-FRIENDLY: No

DOG-FRIENDLY: No

WHEELCHAIR ACCESSIBLE: Yes

EQUIPMENT NEEDED: Casual clothes, bathing suit, walking shoes

COST: Cruises start at $3,745.

ACCESSIBLE BY PUBLIC TRANSPORTATION: Yes

DISTANCE FROM DOWNTOWN PORTLAND: Leaves from waterfront

FACILITIES: *SS Legacy* has an elevator, dining room, lounge, daily yoga, limited exercise equipment, massage, self-serve whiskey bar

SPECIAL COMMENTS: A terrific option for history/nature lovers who don't want to dress for dinner

ON THE THE GROUND

20 HIKE TO WARRIOR ROCK LIGHTHOUSE

Sauvie Island, the largest island in the Columbia River, offers several pleasantly flat hikes. A three-mile trail leads to Warrior Rock, Oregon's smallest working lighthouse. Hikers drive to the end of Reeder Road and then park in the gravel lot. Don't be deterred by the surprising lack of signage. Follow the sandy track along the Columbia and pass through groves of riparian trees, such as cottonwood and ash. A chorus of robins and warblers, the occasional honk of a goose, and the lapping of the Columbia against the shore might be the only sounds you hear during quieter months. River traffic ranges from freighters to sea lions or a cormorant catching a ride on a floating log. At the end of your hike, you'll reach Warrior Rock, so named by Lieutenant William Broughton in 1792, after Chinook warriors in canoes surrounded his party of explorers. The original Warrior Rock Light was built here in 1889.

sauvieisland.org/visitor-information/recreation/hiking

WHEN TO GO: Throughout the year, but heavy rains may flood the trail, especially in spring

HOURS: Daytime

KID-FRIENDLY: Yes

DOG-FRIENDLY: Yes

WHEELCHAIR ACCESSIBLE: No

EQUIPMENT NEEDED: Hiking shoes, binoculars to watch for birds and river life

COST: $10 for parking permit

ACCESSIBLE BY PUBLIC TRANSPORTATION: No

DISTANCE FROM DOWNTOWN PORTLAND: Twenty miles

FACILITIES: Porta-potty at trailhead

SPECIAL COMMENTS: A top place to see migrating birds

21 HIKE THE LOWER MACLEAY PARK TRAIL

When you only have a couple of hours but want to feel that you're out in the forest, hiking the Lower Macleay Park Trail in Forest Park is an ideal choice, giving you that iconic Northwest look right in town. All the necessary elements are there—joyful, burbling Balch Creek, lush Douglas fir forest, a carpet of ferns, and a real unpaved trail that climbs upward but isn't too hard. Almost a mile in, everybody, especially kids, likes to stop and admire the ruins of the Stone House that marks the junction with the Wildwood Trail. The City of Portland built the structure, nicknamed the Witch's Castle for its fairy-tale look, as a comfort station in 1929. Farther up the trail, hikers can stop off at the Audubon Society of Portland to check out the wild birds it's rehabilitating or continue on up to the giant 1914 Pittock Mansion, Portland's favorite historic home. The panoramic views around the mansion reward hikers for the 2.5-mile climb.

NW Twenty-Ninth Avenue and NW Upshur Street

WHEN TO GO: Year-round, but be prepared for mud in the rainy season

HOURS: 5:00 a.m. to 11:00 p.m.; daylight is best

KID-FRIENDLY: Yes

DOG-FRIENDLY: Yes

WHEELCHAIR ACCESSIBLE: No

EQUIPMENT NEEDED: Good shoes, water

COST: Free, but bring money ($10 adults, $7 children) if you want to tour the Pittock Mansion

ACCESSIBLE BY PUBLIC TRANSPORTATION: Yes

DISTANCE FROM DOWNTOWN PORTLAND: Three miles

FACILITIES: Restrooms

SPECIAL COMMENTS: This trail is very busy. Weekdays and early morning may be less trafficked.

22 CLIMB COUNCIL CREST

There are many ways to climb Council Crest—by foot, bike, car, or bus. In the first half of the twentieth century, Portlanders rode a streetcar and then climbed the last stretch on a wooden staircase. However they arrived, all came for spectacular views. At 1,073 feet, it's Portland's highest point. Five Cascade Range mountains are visible from Council Crest on a clear day. Besides the views, Council Crest has grassy expanses for relaxing and picnics, a pretty rose garden, an enormous radio tower, and a Frederic Littman statue called *Joy* of a young mother swinging her baby into the air. On a warm day, you might catch a breeze. On a winter day, it's downright cold. John Talbot claimed the crest in 1849, worried about malaria affecting his family and cows in the valley and thinking it "high enough to be healthy." His wisdom has been confirmed. The bikers, hikers, and dog walkers who summit the crest come in search of good health, fresh air, and beauty.

SW Council Crest Dr.

WHEN TO GO: On clear days year-round

HOURS: 5:00 a.m. to midnight; motor vehicles: 8:00 a.m. to 9:00 p.m. April 1–October 31; 8:00 a.m. to 7:00 p.m. November 1–March 31

KID-FRIENDLY: Yes

DOG-FRIENDLY: Yes

WHEELCHAIR ACCESSIBLE: Yes

EQUIPMENT NEEDED: Walking shoes, jacket on windy days

COST: Free, but bring fifty cents to look through the telescope

ACCESSIBLE BY PUBLIC TRANSPORTATION: Yes

DISTANCE FROM DOWNTOWN PORTLAND: Three miles

FACILITIES: None

SPECIAL COMMENTS: Known as a classic Portland makeout spot. Maybe that's why they close it to cars at night?

23 UNLOCK BIKETOWN

Anyone new to Portland will quickly notice the proliferation of bright orange bicycles. These enormously heavy, two-wheeled tanks arrived on the Portland landscape in 2016 and are called Biketown—pronounced "Bikey Town" in honor of sponsor Nike. Portland's bike-sharing program is fairly easy to use. Download the Biketown app, create an account, release your credit card information, sign an exhaustively long waiver, and you're ready to unlock a bike. All the bikes are tracked by GPS, so the app leads riders to the nearest of one thousand bikes at one hundred stations around town. The bikes feature step-through frames and nicely padded seats. They're not fast but are easy to ride and designed for short trips in an urban setting. Many visitors like to try out a Biketown bike on Portland's famously bike-friendly streets, but locals are the heart of the program. As more people move to Portland and the streets jam with traffic, Biketown offers a valuable transportation alternative.

biketownpdx.com
adaptivebiketown.com

WHEN TO GO: Year-round

HOURS: 24/7

KID-FRIENDLY: No, eighteen and up only

DOG-FRIENDLY: No

WHEELCHAIR ACCESSIBLE: No, although Biketown is partnering with Kerr Bikes for hourly rentals of hand-powered and other adaptive bikes

EQUIPMENT NEEDED: Helmet

COST: A thirty-minute single ride is $2.50. An annual pass costs $12/month.

ACCESSIBLE BY PUBLIC TRANSPORTATION: Varies

DISTANCE FROM DOWNTOWN PORTLAND: Varies

FACILITIES: None

SPECIAL COMMENTS: If you lose the bike, it costs $1,500, so be sure to bring the U-lock provided and lock the bike properly.

24 TAKE A SEGWAY TOUR OF VANCOUVER

Riding a Segway is a strange, gliding experience on an intuitive machine that mind melds with the rider. Lean forward, it goes forward. Lean backward, back it goes. Its handlebars are as receptive as a steering wheel. For those yearning to experience these futuristic devices, you can't beat Ray Bouvier, aka Segway Ray, as a guide. He's such a joke-loving, storytelling extrovert that it's hard to believe he was an actuary back when he used to "ride a desk," as he puts it. In 2013, he and his wife, Tracy, followed their true calling—founding a Segway tour business and showing folks around Vancouver, Washington. Tours start at Fort Vancouver National Historic Site. Routes vary according to the group's interests. Likely stops include Pearson Field, the Waterfront Renaissance Trail along the Columbia River, public art in downtown Vancouver, and the Vancouver Land Bridge. Groups are small—no more than six— and Ray encourages everybody to go at their own pace to get that effortless, magical gliding feeling.

612 E Reserve St., Vancouver
360-693-2939
ezglidetours.com/EZgt/Welcome.html

WHEN TO GO: Year-round

HOURS: Varies. Contact Ray to set up or join a tour.

KID-FRIENDLY: Twelve and up, must be accompanied by licensed adult over twenty-one

DOG-FRIENDLY: No

WHEELCHAIR ACCESSIBLE: No

EQUIPMENT NEEDED: Credit card to secure rental agreement

COST: $75 per person for ninety-minute tour; $85 for two hours

ACCESSIBLE BY PUBLIC TRANSPORTATION: Yes

DISTANCE FROM DOWNTOWN PORTLAND: Nine miles

FACILITIES: Restrooms open during park hours, closed Sunday

SPECIAL COMMENTS: Sensible shoes are a must! Wear your sneakers.

25 DO THE 4T TRAIL

This innovative urban hike shows off Portland's public transportation. The premise of the 4T Trail is gimmicky but fun. Tour Portland on 4 Ts: train, trail, tram, and trolley. Riders start by catching the MAX light rail train downtown. They ride it to Washington Park, where they follow signs to the second T, about three miles of trails. Walkers climb to Council Crest, Portland's highest point at 1,073 feet. After taking in the view, they continue down through Marquam Nature Park and some hilly neighborhood streets until they reach Oregon Health Sciences University. Cutting through the hospital leads hikers to the tram station. The tram provides excellent eastward views as it glides down toward the Willamette River. At the base of the hill, round a corner to board the Portland Streetcar, a.k.a. "trolley," to fulfill the fourth T. The trolley takes riders back to near where they started. The 4T is a fun and inexpensive outing for folks who like to explore on foot and by public transportation.

library.oregonmetro.gov/files/trailtramtrolleytrain.pdf

WHEN TO GO: Dryer weather, unless you like muddy trails

HOURS: Daytime

KID-FRIENDLY: No

DOG-FRIENDLY: No

WHEELCHAIR ACCESSIBLE: No

EQUIPMENT NEEDED: Walking shoes

COST: $5 for a TriMet day pass

ACCESSIBLE BY PUBLIC TRANSPORTATION: Yes

DISTANCE FROM DOWNTOWN PORTLAND: Starts downtown

FACILITIES: Restrooms in Washington Park and at OHSU

SPECIAL COMMENTS: Check the tram schedule, as it has shorter hours than the MAX or trolley.

26 BIKE OR WALK ACROSS TILIKUM CROSSING

Because the Willamette River bisects Portland, dividing it into the East Side and West Side, the city's dozen bridges are vital. In 2015, the city welcomed a special new car-free bridge only open to cyclists, pedestrians, and public transportation. The 1,720-foot Tilikum Crossing bridge boasts a fourteen-foot cycle and walking path on each side. Buses, streetcars, and light-rail trains run down the middle. It's a pretty, white bridge with two 180-foot towers and 178 LED lights that change colors based on the river's height, speed, and temperature. In the year leading up to the bridge's opening, the Bridge Naming Committee received more than nine thousand submissions. It ultimately chose a word from the Chinook Wawa language that means people, tribe, or relatives. Many cyclists focused on efficiency still pedal over the more central bridges to get to work downtown, but those out for a leisurely or scenic ride revel in not having to share the bridge with Portland's ever-increasing number of motorists.

portlandoregon.gov/transportation/68548

WHEN TO GO: Any time

HOURS: 24/7

KID-FRIENDLY: Yes

DOG-FRIENDLY: Yes

WHEELCHAIR ACCESSIBLE: Yes

EQUIPMENT NEEDED: Walking shoes, bike, or transit ticket

COST: Free

ACCESSIBLE BY PUBLIC TRANSPORTATION: Yes

DISTANCE FROM DOWNTOWN PORTLAND: Two miles

FACILITIES: None

SPECIAL COMMENTS: A nice side trip if you're cycling the Springwater Corridor Trail along the Willamette River

27 HIKE WITH THE MAZAMAS

Portland's nonprofit mountaineering education organization was founded by 105 members in 1894. Now it has more than 3,500 members and offers 1,000+ hikes and climbs every year. The Mazamas offers the perfect opportunity for people looking for hiking and climbing buddies, including newbies, and you don't have to be a member to participate. The easiest way to check out the Mazamas is to join it for a hike or city ramble. Its website lists all its adventures coded by difficulty and pace. Choose your hike, show up at the designated place and time, sign in, pay your small participation fee, carpool to the trailhead, and you're off hiking with your new friends. Street rambles explore Portland neighborhoods and trails, while hikes could take you on an easy river trail or a steep climb up a nearby mountain. This organization has thrived for more than a century because of the camaraderie forged on the trails.

527 SE Forty-Third Ave.
503-227-2345
mazamas.org

WHEN TO GO: Year-round

HOURS: Varies

KID-FRIENDLY: Some, with advance notice to hike leader

DOG-FRIENDLY: Generally no

WHEELCHAIR ACCESSIBLE: No

EQUIPMENT NEEDED: The ten essentials: whistle, map, compass, sun protection, headlamp, extra food and water, extra clothing, fire starter, first aid kit, repair kit, and emergency shelter

COST: Hikes are $4 for nonmembers, $2 for members

ACCESSIBLE BY PUBLIC TRANSPORTATION: Street rambles and in-town hikes, yes

DISTANCE FROM DOWNTOWN PORTLAND: Varies

FACILITIES: No

SPECIAL COMMENTS: The Mazamas website has a lot of information. Give yourself time to read it carefully.

28 JOIN A PEDALPALOOZA EVENT

Portland loves bikes, and its decentralized bike festival, Pedalpalooza, grows every year. Pedalpalooza evolved out of a 2002 event called Bike Summer and now features about three hundred Pedalpalooza-associated bike activities stretching through the month of June. Volunteer leaders pick a theme and post their rides on the event's website. Interested citizens show up with their bikes. Some rides are easy to understand, such as a heritage tree ride around Vancouver or a ginger ride for redheads. Others are more enigmatic, and you'll have to show up to find out exactly what goes on. Many rides feature costumes, music, and stops for doughnuts or beer. Pedalpalooza's climax is the annual Naked Bike Ride, which draws more than ten thousand nudies to cycle the streets of Portland. The point of Pedalpalooza is to boost bike riding and decrease Portlanders' dependence on cars and fossil fuels. For bike lovers, this is a fabulous community event that lets them take over city streets with like-minded cyclists.

820 SW Second Ave., Suite 200
shift2bikes.org

WHEN TO GO: June

HOURS: Varies

KID-FRIENDLY: Some rides are; check website

DOG-FRIENDLY: No

WHEELCHAIR ACCESSIBLE: No

EQUIPMENT NEEDED: Bike, helmet, water

COST: Free, but the organizing body accepts donations.

ACCESSIBLE BY PUBLIC TRANSPORTATION: Varies

DISTANCE FROM DOWNTOWN PORTLAND: Varies

FACILITIES: Varies

SPECIAL COMMENTS: Wear a helmet, even to the Naked Bike Ride.

29 EXPLORE POWELL BUTTE NATURE PARK

Portland stores one hundred million gallons of water beneath Powell Butte. Two thousand miles of pipes running from the underground reservoir make this extinct volcanic cinder cone the hub of the city's water system. The nature park plays up this water aspect with visitor center displays of a water flow model, the city's original wooden pipes, and some iron relics put into service in 1883. An artistic patio display compares the circumference of different water pipes. People who like to know how things work will love the visitors center, but people mostly come for the variety of excellently marked trails—your choice of open meadow or forest, paved or narrow dirt and travel by bike, foot, or horse. On a clear day, visitors get perfect views of Mount Hood and Mount Saint Helens and glimpses of Jefferson, Adams, and Rainier. Spring brings masses of wildflowers. In the summer, breezes carry the smell of drying flowers and ripening berries and gently rustle the whole meadow.

16160 SE Powell Blvd.
503-823-2223
portlandoregon.gov/parks/finder/index.
cfm?action=ViewPark&PropertyID=528

WHEN TO GO: Year-round

HOURS: Opens 7:00 a.m.; closing time ranges from 6:00 p.m. to 10:00 p.m. by season.

KID-FRIENDLY: Yes

DOG-FRIENDLY: Yes

WHEELCHAIR ACCESSIBLE: Visitors center and Mountain View Trail; motorized wheelchair or assistance might be required for hill.

EQUIPMENT NEEDED: Walking shoes

COST: Free

ACCESSIBLE BY PUBLIC TRANSPORTATION: Yes

DISTANCE FROM DOWNTOWN PORTLAND: Thirteen miles

FACILITIES: Restroom

SPECIAL COMMENTS: Stay aware of closing time or your car could be gated in the lot overnight.

30 EXPLORE OAKS BOTTOM WILDLIFE REFUGE

Oaks Bottom conveniently offers nature lovers a mix of the mossy logs and ferns of Oregon's forests and views of the Willamette River without even having to leave the city. This 168-acre parcel of land in Southeast Portland has been protected since 1988, keeping these wetlands safe for herons to nest, beavers to build dams, and Portlanders to walk their dogs. Long ago Native Americans came here to gather a potato-like edible root called *wapato* and to fish for salmon. Nowadays, you'll see people fishing in modern boats. It's a strange sensation to walk along sections of the path and feel forest solitude, and then the trail turns and you glimpse a downtown skyscraper or a flash of color as a neon-clad biker races by on the Springwater Corridor, which runs through Oaks Bottom. From mid-February through June, more than a hundred great blue herons—Portland's official city bird—nest here, fishing for carp to feed their young. The trails are easy and mostly flat.

SE Milwaukie Ave. & SE Mitchell St.
503-823-7529

WHEN TO GO: Year-round

HOURS: Daylight

KID-FRIENDLY: Yes

DOG-FRIENDLY: Yes

WHEELCHAIR ACCESSIBLE: Only the beginning paved stretch of the trail

EQUIPMENT NEEDED: Walking shoes

COST: Free

ACCESSIBLE BY PUBLIC TRANSPORTATION: Yes

DISTANCE FROM DOWNTOWN PORTLAND: Five miles

FACILITIES: Porta-potty

SPECIAL COMMENTS: Trails can be very muddy. Wear good boots if it's rained recently.

31 CYCLE THE BANKS-VERNONIA TRAIL

While most popular with cyclists, the shady Banks-Vernonia Trail also welcomes walkers, runners, and horseback riders to the Coast Range foothills. The twenty-one-mile out-and-back trail has a special place in Oregon outdoor recreation history as the state's first "rail to trails" project. Trains carried logs from Vernonia's lumber mills to Portland along this route in the 1920s. After the mill closed in 1957, an excursion train operated briefly before the tracks were abandoned. In 1991, building started on the present trail. Cyclists now start at Banks and enjoy a few flat miles of Washington County farmland before a slight upward grade through a forest of alders, Douglas firs, maples, and cedars. Except for one hill, the grade remains gentle. Highlights include two eighty-foot railroad trestles and thirteen bridges. Bikers who complete the full twenty-one miles to Vernonia often stop for lunch—the restaurants have plenty of bike parking. Fans of the *Twilight* vampire series might recognize the town as a setting in the films.

Manning Trailhead: NW Pihl Rd, Banks   503-324-0606

WHEN TO GO: Year-round

HOURS: Daytime

KID-FRIENDLY: Yes, and you don't have to ride the full forty-two miles

DOG-FRIENDLY: Yes

WHEELCHAIR ACCESSIBLE: Yes

EQUIPMENT NEEDED: Bike or walking shoes, water, snacks

COST: Free

ACCESSIBLE BY PUBLIC TRANSPORTATION: No

DISTANCE FROM DOWNTOWN PORTLAND: Thirty-one miles

FACILITIES: Restroom at trailhead

SPECIAL COMMENTS: Expect many cyclists on nice days, including unpredictable children, so go slowly and enjoy the views.

32 PEDAL THE OREGON COAST ON TRAIN TRACKS

A cross between biking and taking a scenic train ride, railriding involves pedaling four-person carts down old railroad tracks. You can do this only a few places around the country, and one of them is with Oregon Coast Railriders, ninety minutes west of Portland. The owners, bike tourism promoters and entrepreneurs Kim and Anita Metlen, operate the popular Joseph Branch Railriders in eastern Oregon. They expanded their operation to Bay City in 2016. Railriding is more relaxing than biking, as nothing else runs on this stretch of track, and guides stop traffic at road crossings. While pedaling the relatively flat twelve-mile route, riders take in views of Tillamook Bay, estuaries, meadows, and native coastal plants, and cross two railroad bridges more than two hundred years old. A bald eagle might cruise overhead. As manager Nate Bell puts it, the two-hour ride is 80 percent scenic and 20 percent reality—the reality being the close-up views—and smells—of Tillamook County's massive dairy operations.

5400 Hayes Oyster Dr., Bay City
541-786-6165
ocrailriders.com

WHEN TO GO: May–October 2

HOURS: Thursday–Monday, three tours per day at 9:00 a.m., noon, and 3:00 p.m.

KID-FRIENDLY: Yes. Babies and toddlers require car seats, and you should arrive forty minutes early.

DOG-FRIENDLY: No

WHEELCHAIR ACCESSIBLE: No

EQUIPMENT NEEDED: Tours run rain or shine, so bring sunscreen, hat, rain gear, depending

COST: $22 for adults, $10 for children under twelve

ACCESSIBLE BY PUBLIC TRANSPORTATION: Yes

DISTANCE FROM DOWNTOWN PORTLAND: Seventy-eight miles

FACILITIES: Porta-potty; gift store selling hats, T-shirts, and water

SPECIAL COMMENTS: Weight limit is 280 pounds. Reserve ahead, especially for groups. Arrive thirty minutes early so that the tour can leave on time.

33 RUN ON A TRACK

On the excitement spectrum, running on a track falls between treadmills and trails, but track running has its advantages— joint-friendly surfaces, freedom from stopping for or worrying about traffic, outside air, and easily measurable distances. Portland has many well-maintained tracks that are open to the public. A soccer or lacrosse practice is often going on in the middle of the track, giving runners a welcome distraction from burning lungs and hamstrings. In East Portland, the track at Floyd Light Middle School is set back from streets and features views of mature trees in adjacent Floyd Light Park. In Northeast Portland, Grant High School has Nike to thank for its dazzling turf field. Meanwhile, in Southwest Portland, Under Armour donated a new turf track to Duniway Park in 2016, vexing its sportswear competitor as it replaced a previous track made of recycled Nike shoes. Portlanders lace up their sneakers and take advantage of this largesse at parks and schools all over town, running or walking their way to increased cardiovascular health.

Floyd Light Middle School
10800 SE Washington St.

Grant High School
2245 NE Thirty-Sixth Ave.

Duniway Park
SW Sixth and SW Sheridan St.

WHEN TO GO: Year-round

HOURS: Nonschool hours for school tracks; daylight for parks

KID-FRIENDLY: Yes

DOG-FRIENDLY: No

WHEELCHAIR ACCESSIBLE: Varies; wheelchair tires damage some types of track.

EQUIPMENT NEEDED: Running shoes

COST: Free

ACCESSIBLE BY PUBLIC TRANSPORTATION: Yes

DISTANCE FROM DOWNTOWN PORTLAND: Varies

FACILITIES: Varies

SPECIAL COMMENTS: Generally, four laps equal one mile.

34 BIKE THE SPRINGWATER CORRIDOR

This bike trail started life in 1903 as a railroad that hauled passengers and farm produce around the area. Nicknamed the Springwater Line, the name stuck when the City of Portland acquired it in 1990 and began turning it into a recreational site. Section by section, the city opened the trail to bicyclists, walkers, runners, wheelchairs, and, mostly east of I-205, horseback riders. The 21.5-mile asphalt path now stretches from SE Fourth Avenue all the way to Boring, Oregon, connecting some of Portland's eastside parks and natural areas, such as Oaks Amusement Park, Powell Butte Nature Park, and the Tideman Johnson Natural Area. The stretch running along the Willamette is especially nice—an easy, almost flat ride with river and wetland views, and maybe a glimpse of a raccoon family or other urban wildlife. Vagrant campsites beside the far east parts of the trail have caused problems in recent years, so cyclists might want to stay west of I-205 or ride in a group if venturing in that direction.

SE Ivon Street to Boring
Portland Parks and Recreation: 503-823-7529

WHEN TO GO: Year-round

HOURS: Daylight

KID-FRIENDLY: Yes

DOG-FRIENDLY: Yes

WHEELCHAIR ACCESSIBLE: Yes

EQUIPMENT NEEDED: Walking shoes or bike

COST: Free

ACCESSIBLE BY PUBLIC TRANSPORTATION: Yes

DISTANCE FROM DOWNTOWN PORTLAND: Varies

FACILITIES: None

SPECIAL COMMENTS: Much of the trail is very dark at night, so make sure you have good bike lights and wear a headlamp if riding late.

35 PARTICIPATE IN A $5 FUN RUN

Organizers of 5Ks outdo each other with over-the-top themes, but these often come with a high price tag. Portland Parks and Recreation designed its series of 5Ks to be basic, fun, encouraging, and affordable. During the summer, races are held one Sunday per month, revolving through different parks around the city. Depending on the park, the course will probably be two or three laps around the perimeter. Events start with a 1K kids' run. Runners who expect to finish in twenty-four minutes or less start at 9:00 a.m., while everybody else starts at 9:30 a.m. There's something exhilarating and motivating about running with a pack of local citizens of all ages, even for runners who don't take it too seriously. A typical Parks and Recreation 5K includes an emcee, "Eye of the Tiger" blaring through a loudspeaker, a few local businesses with booths, and, if you're lucky, Dill, a giant pickle mascot who poses for pictures as runners await the starting horn.

503-823-7529
portlandoregon.gov/parks/61144

WHEN TO GO: May to October, one Sunday a month during summer

HOURS: 8:30 a.m. to 11:30 a.m.

KID-FRIENDLY: Yes

DOG-FRIENDLY: No

WHEELCHAIR ACCESSIBLE: No

EQUIPMENT NEEDED: Running shoes

COST: $5; youth seventeen and under free

ACCESSIBLE BY PUBLIC TRANSPORTATION: Yes

DISTANCE FROM DOWNTOWN PORTLAND: Varies

FACILITIES: Porta-potties, water stations, bananas, Gatorade

SPECIAL COMMENTS: Walkers welcome

36 GO CROSS-COUNTRY SKIING AT MOUNT HOOD

Cross-country—also known as Nordic—skiing takes a little more skill than snowshoeing, but it gives you that magical gliding feeling that only comes from skis without the breakneck speed and danger of downhill skiing. Mount Hood offers several groomed trails and equipment rentals. Outdoorsy, sporty people might prefer to rent skis and figure it out on their own. Less confident folks benefit from a guided outing and/or at least one lesson from a ski instructor. Mount Hood Adventure in Government Camp offers guided expeditions with a naturalist who will meet you at the groomed trail at Trillium Lake, give ski tips, share snippets of local history, and point out coyote and snowshoe hare tracks. Most importantly, a guide answers important questions, such as how to avoid hitting trees and how to get back up when you fall with those long skis on your feet. Cross-country skiing gets you out to Mount Hood's back country, enjoying the Douglas fir forest while getting a surprising amount of exercise.

88661 Government Camp Loop Rd., Government Camp
503-715-2175
mounthoodadventure.com

WHEN TO GO: December to April, depending on snowfall

HOURS: Daylight is best for beginners.

KID-FRIENDLY: Yes

DOG-FRIENDLY: No

WHEELCHAIR ACCESSIBLE: No

EQUIPMENT NEEDED: Skis, boots, poles

COST: $25–$30 for rental package. Nordic centers charge track fees of about $15. Lesson prices vary.

ACCESSIBLE BY PUBLIC TRANSPORTATION: Yes, but will take a few hours

DISTANCE FROM DOWNTOWN PORTLAND: Fifty-seven miles

FACILITIES: Mount Hood has several towns and ski areas with lots of lodging and restaurants.

SPECIAL COMMENTS: Leave that heavy coat in the car. You'll get plenty warm while skiing.

37 GO SNOWSHOEING AT MOUNT HOOD

Snowshoeing is the easiest winter sport. It's like walking but with really big feet. It's also the quietest—no neon-clad people whizzing by on a slope, no roar of a snowmobile motor— and the least expensive. So if winter makes you yearn to get outside into a silent white world, snowshoeing is ideal. Mount Hood generally offers the closest snow for Portland people. Beginners should pick marked trails with gentle elevation gains and drops, as navigating steeper slopes is tricky and breaking a trail through new snow is tiring. The Twin Lakes Trail is usually packed down enough to make it easier, and the Old Barlow Road Trail sports dramatic icicles. While snowshoeing poses fewer risks than skiing or snowboarding, it's still wise to go with a buddy or two. Mount Hood Adventures offers snowshoeing tours, including by moonlight, and Portland Community College has a one-day snowshoeing class. Next Adventure's Outdoor School has the best deal—$50 includes gear rental, instruction, a guide, and round-trip transportation from Portland.

Twin Lakes Trail starts at Frog Lake Sno Park
Highway 26, Mount Hood

WHEN TO GO: Winter; check the snow reports at Mount Hood.

HOURS: Daylight for beginners or by moonlight with a guide

KID-FRIENDLY: Yes

DOG-FRIENDLY: Yes

WHEELCHAIR ACCESSIBLE: No

EQUIPMENT NEEDED: Snowshoes, poles can help, warm clothes

COST: You can rent snowshoes at Mount Hood Adventure or Mount Hood Meadows Rental Center for about $15.

ACCESSIBLE BY PUBLIC TRANSPORTATION: Yes, but sparse

DISTANCE FROM DOWNTOWN PORTLAND: Sixty miles

FACILITIES: Mount Hood has towns and resorts with restaurants, shops, and lodging.

SPECIAL COMMENTS: Don't try to snowshoe backward.

Cities around the US host Turkey Trots on Thanksgiving morning, but Portland is one of the very few that offer a vegetarian alternative—the Tofurky Trot. Sponsored by the Hood River-based Turtle Island Foods—known for making that faceless Thanksgiving alterna-bird—this 5K is for plant eaters. Proceeds benefit Northwest VEG, farm sanctuaries, and other pro-animal nonprofits. The winners take home a frozen Tofurky, but for the other 99 percent of runners, this 5K is not competitive enough to warrant chip timing. The cheerful group begins at Oaks Park amusement park and follows a trail through Sellwood, enjoying like-minded camaraderie on a day known for turkey slaughter. The veg gang burns off some calories before presumably eating a large, plant-based dinner. Expect children, dogs, and people dressed up as giant carrots and peas. After the race, runners sample vegan protein bars and drink coffee while they dry off— late November in Portland is typically rainy.

503-746-8344
nwveg.org

WHEN TO GO: Thanksgiving morning

HOURS: 9:00 a.m. to noon

KID-FRIENDLY: Yes

DOG-FRIENDLY: Well-behaved, on a leash

WHEELCHAIR ACCESSIBLE: Possibly, depending on route. Contact race organizers ahead.

EQUIPMENT NEEDED: Running shoes, layered clothing, rain gear

COST: $25

ACCESSIBLE BY PUBLIC TRANSPORTATION: Yes

DISTANCE FROM DOWNTOWN PORTLAND: Five miles

FACILITIES: Restrooms, snacks

SPECIAL COMMENTS: Walkers are welcome too.

39 BIKE OR WALK THE SUNDAY PARKWAYS

Since 2008, this bike and pedestrian takeover of neighborhood streets has drawn thousands of people of all ages. For four or five summertime Sundays, select routes are closed to motorized traffic. Organizers make sure different areas of Portland are represented. For example, one year's event might include six- to ten-mile routes in Southeast Portland, Sellwood, North Portland, Northeast Portland, and Outer Northeast Portland. Neighborhood parks along the way provide hubs of food carts and entertainment, with restroom facilities and places to rest. This is a very family-friendly event, with lots of young children biking unpredictably, so participants need to stay patient and alert and not expect a racing event. Sunday Parkways relies on hundreds of volunteers. Even if you don't like biking in a crowd, you can get involved by volunteering to monitor an intersection or hand out water and snacks. Or just hang out in one of the parks and enjoy the bands, buy a burrito, or participate in a Zumba demo.

portlandoregon.gov/transportation/46103

WHEN TO GO: One Sunday afternoon during each summer month

HOURS: 11:00 a.m. to 4:00 p.m.

KID-FRIENDLY: Yes

DOG-FRIENDLY: With walkers or runners, on a leash

WHEELCHAIR ACCESSIBLE: Yes

EQUIPMENT NEEDED: Sneakers, bike, helmet, sunscreen, water bottle

COST: Free

ACCESSIBLE BY PUBLIC TRANSPORTATION: Yes

DISTANCE FROM DOWNTOWN PORTLAND: Varies

FACILITIES: Porta-potties, food carts

SPECIAL COMMENTS: A very Portland experience

40 RUN THE STARLIGHT PARADE COURSE

Most people will never experience the roar of a quarter million fans urging them on for their athletic exploits. This acclaim is usually reserved for Olympic athletes and NFL players, but at the Starlight Run you can enjoy this level of positive reinforcement even if you run a fourteen-minute mile. The annual race precedes the Starlight Parade, one of the highlights of Portland's Rose Festival. About 250,000 people descend upon downtown, arriving many hours before the parade to secure a spot. So when the 5K runners pass, the people in lawn chairs lining the parade route put down their Doritos to clap and cheer. Kids line up to give the runners high fives. Runners try to outdo each other with the most creative and colorful getups to win the costume contest. You won't find such a supportive 5K experience anywhere else. The event ends with refreshments and entertainment at Lincoln High School, but runners usually hurry back to see the parade's elaborately decorated, electrified floats.

Starting point: Lincoln High School
SW Sixteenth Avenue and SW Salmon Street
rosefestival.org/event/starlight-run

WHEN TO GO: On the Saturday of the annual Starlight Parade

HOURS: Race starts at 7:45 a.m.

KID-FRIENDLY: Yes

DOG-FRIENDLY: No

WHEELCHAIR ACCESSIBLE: No

EQUIPMENT NEEDED: Running shoes, costume

COST: $20

ACCESSIBLE BY PUBLIC TRANSPORTATION: Yes

DISTANCE FROM DOWNTOWN PORTLAND: Downtown

FACILITIES: Porta-potties; expect long lines

SPECIAL COMMENTS: Because of parade route restrictions, participants must be able to maintain a pace of at least fourteen minutes per mile; no walkers allowed.

41 HIKE THROUGH TUALATIN HILLS NATURE PARK

This 222-acre West Side nature park is good for a flat stroll on paved or unpaved trails through Douglas firs, white oaks, ponderosa pines, and masses of sword fern. The compact five-mile trail system takes visitors through forests and wetlands. Look for ducks, frogs, and dragonflies in Big Pond and Lily Pond. In springtime, wildflowers bloom, and rough-skinned newts scurry across the trails as they migrate to breeding ponds. A visitors center educates with fun displays, including microscopes to examine owl pellets, leaves, and other things found around the park, and a giant model of a banana slug. Children will enjoy gross-out slug fun facts, such as learning about two types of predator-gagging slug slime—one to lubricate movement, the other to prevent slipping on vertical surfaces. The park hosts special events, such as Newt Day and native plant sales. These short trails are perfect for introducing young children to hiking or for walkers and runners of all ages to complete a flat, pretty, car-free five miles.

15655 SW Millikan Way, Beaverton
thprd.org/parks-and-trails/detail/tualatin-hills-nature-park

WHEN TO GO: Year-round

HOURS: Daily, dawn to dusk

KID-FRIENDLY: Yes

DOG-FRIENDLY: No

WHEELCHAIR ACCESSIBLE: Limited: Oak Trail and parts of Vine Maple Trail

EQUIPMENT NEEDED: Sneakers

COST: Free

ACCESSIBLE BY PUBLIC TRANSPORTATION: Yes

DISTANCE FROM DOWNTOWN PORTLAND: Ten miles

FACILITIES: Restrooms, water fountain, visitors center with gift shop

SPECIAL COMMENTS: Very close to MAX station, for those who like to take public transportation to their trailhead

FLORA

AND

FAUNA

42 BIRD-WATCH AT SAUVIE ISLAND

Ten miles north of Portland, the flat, open expanse of Sauvie Island sits in the Columbia River. At fifteen miles long and four miles wide, this island is similar in size to Manhattan. Farmers grow berries, peaches, flowers, herbs, corn, and many other vegetables on the island's southern half. The north half is a wildlife refuge. And everywhere? Birds. More than 250 species of birds live here or migrate through. Dedicated birders will enjoy differentiating the song of a nuthatch from that of a chickadee, but even the avian-ignorant will be wowed by the sight of a thousand sandhill cranes dancing and purring in the hacked-off winter remains of a cornfield or the bright white dots of snow geese contrasting with green springtime grass. Several viewing platforms around the island are designated birdwatching spots, but you're likely to see flocks gathering at any field or watering hole just off the roads. The Audubon Society offers naturalist-led trips, or visitors can poke around on their own.

503-292-6855

sauvieisland.org/visitor-information/recreation/bird-watching

WHEN TO GO: Year-round, with different avian guest stars each month

HOURS: Daytime

KID-FRIENDLY: Yes

DOG-FRIENDLY: Legal on leash but could make the birds nervous

WHEELCHAIR ACCESSIBLE: The viewing points at Howell Territorial Park, Coon Point, and the Wildlife Viewing Platform are wheelchair accessible.

EQUIPMENT NEEDED: Binoculars, hiking shoes, daily parking permit

COST: $10 for parking permit

ACCESSIBLE BY PUBLIC TRANSPORTATION: No

DISTANCE FROM DOWNTOWN PORTLAND: Twelve miles

FACILITIES: Porta-potties at designated viewing areas

SPECIAL COMMENTS: This is an easy introduction to birdwatching.

43 STROLL THE OREGON GARDEN

Plant lovers will want to visit the Oregon Garden in every season. One theme area flows into the next as visitors explore oddly shaped trees and shrubs in the Conifer Garden and then ring a rusty temple bell and feel the silky trunk of a paperbark cherry in the Sensory Garden. The Pet-Friendly Garden explores landscaping that's good for gardeners' furry friends and features a statue of Bobbie the Wonder Dog, a famous Silverton native who walked 2,551 miles home after getting lost on a 1923 family camping trip in Indiana. The Children's Garden entertains with a crawl-through tunnel and a sandbox where children can unearth faux dinosaur bones. Summer activities include art shows and outdoor movie nights. Visitors staying at the adjacent Oregon Garden Resort can access the garden before and after public hours. A peaceful stroll in the morning, admiring vibrant pink dahlias and catching a glimpse of a jackrabbit's long ears, might inspire visitors to improve their own patches of land.

879 W Main St., Silverton
503-874-8100
oregongarden.org

WHEN TO GO: Year-round

HOURS: Open daily, 9:00 a.m. to 6:00 p.m., May–Sept; check website for days and hours in other seasons

KID-FRIENDLY: Yes

DOG-FRIENDLY: Yes

WHEELCHAIR ACCESSIBLE: Yes

EQUIPMENT NEEDED: Walking shoes, camera

COST: Adults, $8–$14, children ages five to eleven, $2–$8, depending on the season

ACCESSIBLE BY PUBLIC TRANSPORTATION: Yes

DISTANCE FROM DOWNTOWN PORTLAND: Forty-two miles

FACILITIES: Restrooms, café, gift shop

SPECIAL COMMENTS: A tram runs through the garden if that suits you better than walking.

44 CELEBRATE SPRINGTIME AT CRYSTAL SPRINGS RHODODENDRON GARDEN

For much of the year, Crystal Springs is a quiet place to walk amidst greenery and observe the many types of ducks that make Portland their seasonal home, but from March through June, when rhododendrons puff out in all their red, pink, purple, and white glory, visitors swarm the gardens. Tucked away in a quiet residential neighborhood near Reed College, the 9.5-acre garden has paved and unpaved paths, several bridges, and waterfalls. A dedication plaque from the American Rhododendron Society celebrates Crystal Springs' 1950 beginning in language as flowery as the garden: "While world wars flared and flagged there grew and flourished in Eastmoreland two handsome rhododendron specimens of the variety named Cynthia . . . annually were a delight to thousands; they who lived nearby, and they who sojourned from afar to behold." These original two Cynthias have since been joined by 2,500 other rhodies and azaleas. Bufflehead ducks, green-backed herons, and other waterfowl cruise the pond. An occasional hissing, charging goose adds an element of excitement to otherwise tranquil grounds.

5801 SE Twenty-Eighth Ave.
503-771-8386

WHEN TO GO: Year-round; March to June for blooms; Mother's Day for the biggest party

HOURS: April 1–September 30: 6:00 a.m. to 10:00 p.m.; October 1–March 31: 6:00 a.m. to 6:00 p.m.

KID-FRIENDLY: Yes

DOG-FRIENDLY: Yes

WHEELCHAIR ACCESSIBLE: Yes, on paved trails

EQUIPMENT NEEDED: Walking shoes, camera

COST: Free September 1–February 28; $5 admission charged 10:00 a.m. to 6:00 p.m., Wednesday through Sunday, March 1–August 31

ACCESSIBLE BY PUBLIC TRANSPORTATION: Yes

DISTANCE FROM DOWNTOWN PORTLAND: Five miles

FACILITIES: Restrooms

SPECIAL COMMENTS: A beautiful place for weddings; please don't feed the birds, and especially don't feed them bread.

45 BOOST YOUR TREE SMARTS AT THE HOYT ARBORETUM

Almost any plant can grow in Portland, and the Hoyt Arboretum in Washington Park is a testament to that fact. Eleven hundred species from around the world thrive on Hoyt's 187 acres. Once a poor farm, the arboretum is now a quiet sanctuary for trees, with twelve miles of trails for visitors to explore. Some of the trails are named for the predominant type of tree they pass through, such as spruce, fir, or bristlecone pine, which are planted in organized groups for research purposes. Trail distances range from a half mile to five miles. Pick up a map at the visitors center and wander on your own, or join a group tour on Saturdays during summer. The arboretum changes with the seasons—flowering in spring, colorful in fall—and covers enough territory that one can easily get lost. Each tree was grown from seeds collected in the wild, and its provenance was carefully documented for scientific use, with records dating all the way back to 1914.

4000 SW Fairview Blvd.

503-865-8733   hoytarboretum.org

WHEN TO GO: Year-round

HOURS: 5:00 a.m. to 9:30 p.m.; visitors center: Mon–Fri, 9:00 a.m. to 4:00 p.m.; Sat–Sun, 11:00 a.m. to 3:00 p.m.

KID-FRIENDLY: Yes

DOG-FRIENDLY: Yes

WHEELCHAIR ACCESSIBLE: Two miles of trail are accessible for wheelchairs and strollers.

EQUIPMENT NEEDED: Walking shoes

COST: Free, $3 for group tour

ACCESSIBLE BY PUBLIC TRANSPORTATION: Yes

DISTANCE FROM DOWNTOWN PORTLAND: Three miles

FACILITIES: Restrooms, visitors center

SPECIAL COMMENTS: No bikes are allowed in the arboretum.

46 VISIT THE AUDUBON SANCTUARY

The Audubon Society of Portland owns a 150-acre nature sanctuary adjacent to Forest Park. Because Audubon is pretty much *the* word on birds, you know these four miles of trails are beautiful, well-kept, and inviting for avian friends. Visitors stroll through mixed conifer forest on the banks of Balch Creek, watching for mourning doves, jays, and chickadees. Cutthroat trout live in the creek, and Pacific giant salamanders and roughskin newts poke around in the mud. The on-site Wildlife Care Center, Oregon's oldest wildlife rehab operation, treats thousands of wildlife injuries annually. Visitors can see some of the center's patients, plus a few permanent residents that were too damaged to return to the wild. These "education birds" include Ruby, a turkey vulture of mysterious origins that imprinted on humans rather than other vultures, and Aristophanes the raven, illegally taken from his nest as a chick. The society offers bird-themed classes, field trips, walks, speakers, and activities for children and adults.

5151 NW Cornell Rd.
503-292-6855   audubonportland.org

WHEN TO GO: Year-round

HOURS: Sanctuary trails: dawn to dusk daily; care center, 9:00 a.m. to 5:00 p.m. daily

KID-FRIENDLY: Yes

DOG-FRIENDLY: No

WHEELCHAIR ACCESSIBLE: Care center, yes; trails, no

EQUIPMENT NEEDED: Walking shoes

COST: Free

ACCESSIBLE BY PUBLIC TRANSPORTATION: No

DISTANCE FROM DOWNTOWN PORTLAND: Four miles

FACILITIES: Restroom, gift shop

SPECIAL COMMENTS: Audubon loves volunteers. Consider donating some time on December 31 to help with the annual Christmas bird count.

47 STROLL THE PORTLAND JAPANESE GARDEN

When visiting Portland, a former Japanese ambassador to the US proclaimed this garden "the most beautiful and authentic Japanese garden in the world outside Japan." The garden maintains its serene, timeless feel despite heavy visitor traffic. Visitors wander the dirt and stone trails, discovering a stone bench tucked into a peaceful corner or a pagoda lantern sculpture set among ferns and moss. Four dozen iridescent koi glide in a large pond, each pattern of orange, gold, black, and white more stunning than the last. Staff members call each koi by name and can point out the old man fish, now in his thirties. In a major 2017 renovation, the garden added the Umami Café and a cultural building with an art gallery, library, and classroom, where visitors learn about tea, flower arranging, Kabuki theater, music, and other aspects of Japanese culture. Floor-to-ceiling windows in the café let gardengoers drink tea and eat matcha brownies while gazing over a vista of trees and the garden.

611 SW Kingston Ave.
503-223-1321   japanesegarden.org

WHEN TO GO: Year-round

HOURS: Monday, noon to 7:00 p.m., Tuesday–Sunday, 10:00 a.m. to 7:00 p.m.; winter: Monday, noon to 4:00 p.m., Tuesday–Sunday, 10:00 a.m. to 4:00 p.m.

KID-FRIENDLY: Yes

DOG-FRIENDLY: No

WHEELCHAIR ACCESSIBLE: Limited

EQUIPMENT NEEDED: Walking shoes, camera

COST: Adults, $14.95; seniors (sixty-five and older), $12.95; youth (six to seventeen), $10.45; five and under, free

ACCESSIBLE BY PUBLIC TRANSPORTATION: Yes

DISTANCE FROM DOWNTOWN PORTLAND: Two miles

FACILITIES: Restrooms, café, gift shop

SPECIAL COMMENTS: Get here early in summer to avoid crowds.

48 COUNT SALMON ON THE FISH LADDERS AT BONNEVILLE DAM

Salmon are a keystone species of the Pacific Northwest; if they disappear, the whole ecosystem fails. But salmon have tough lives. Born in fresh water, they migrate to the ocean and then follow their noses back home to spawn and die—some as far as nine hundred miles. Meanwhile, every creature from eagles to sea lions to humans tries to eat them. To add trials to their tribulations, the Army Corps of Engineers built giant dams along the Columbia River for hydropower and navigation. Fish ladders are a concession to salmon's need to circumvent the dams. They look like staircases, with long steps between risers. For fish, it's like a series of ascending pools. They rally their strength to leap through a short cascade of rushing water and then rest in a pool until they're ready to take on the next step. Visitors can check out the ladders from above to understand the layout and then enter the visitors center, where underwater windows provide a peek into this determined fish's travails.

Bradford Island Visitor Center, Star Route, Cascade Locks
541-374-8820   nwp.usace.army.mil/bonneville

WHEN TO GO: Year-round. Chinook count peaks in September

HOURS: 9:00 a.m. to 5:00 p.m.

KID-FRIENDLY: Yes

DOG-FRIENDLY: Not inside visitor center

WHEELCHAIR ACCESSIBLE: Yes

COST: Free

ACCESSIBLE BY PUBLIC TRANSPORTATION: Yes

DISTANCE FROM DOWNTOWN PORTLAND: Forty-three miles

FACILITIES: Restrooms, gift shop

SPECIAL COMMENTS: For more fishy fun, including seeing the eighty-year-old, five-hundred-pound Herman the Sturgeon, check out nearby Bonneville Fish Hatchery.

49 WATCH SWIFTS AT CHAPMAN SCHOOL

Up to two thousand people gather on the dry grass outside Chapman Elementary School in Northwest Portland, eyes glued to the sky. "They're going in!" cries one spectator. "No, it's a fake," says another. Every night in September, up to eight thousand swifts en route to Central America and Venezuela roost overnight in the Chapman School's huge brick chimney. As darkness approaches, they whirl through the air, now resembling a black twister, then breaking apart into separate phalanxes. Because there are so many birds and the chimney opening is relatively small, their descent is a long, graceful process, with much aerial drama. When the last swifts spiral into the chimney, the crowd cheers and applauds. The swifts started using the Chapman chimney in the 1980s. Students and staff responded by bundling up so as not to cook any swifts until the school eventually raised funds for a separate heating system for humans. Swift watching is a Portland tradition, including polite dogs, rambunctious kids, and picnicking.

1445 NW Twenty-Sixth Ave.
audubonportland.org/local-birding/swiftwatch

WHEN TO GO: September

HOURS: 6:00 p.m. to 8:00 p.m., depending on sunset

KID-FRIENDLY: Yes

DOG-FRIENDLY: Yes

WHEELCHAIR ACCESSIBLE: Yes

EQUIPMENT NEEDED: Blankets, lawn chairs, snacks

COST: Free

ACCESSIBLE BY PUBLIC TRANSPORTATION: Yes, and a good choice because parking is tight here

DISTANCE FROM DOWNTOWN PORTLAND: Two miles

FACILITIES: None

SPECIAL COMMENTS: The Audubon Society of Portland needs volunteer swift counters every year if you want to get more involved.

50 BIRD-WATCH AT SMITH AND BYBEE WETLANDS NATURAL AREA

In the far reaches of industrial North Portland, the Smith and Bybee Wetlands Natural Area covers almost two thousand acres, making it the largest protected freshwater wetland in the country. The paved, flat Interlake Trail gives walkers a close-up look at Smith Lake and Bybee Lake. The latter lake changes water level with the tides, making it the best place to view birds. More than one hundred species frequent the wetlands. Great blue herons nest here, despite jets rumbling overhead, while peregrine falcons scan the marshes for prey. People launch canoes and kayaks, depending on the water level, which varies from flood level in winter to downright boggy in summer heat. Watch closely and you might see a muskrat or a Western painted turtle swim by—this is home to one of Oregon's largest populations of the shy creatures. Shell and fish-shaped concrete artworks by artists Valerie Otani and Fernanda D'Agostino dot the edges of the area, bridging the gap between wetlands and the traffic and industry of nearby Marine Drive.

5300 N Marine Dr.   oregonmetro.gov/news/field-guide-smith-bybee-wetlands

WHEN TO GO: Year-round
HOURS: Daylight
KID-FRIENDLY: Yes
DOG-FRIENDLY: No
WHEELCHAIR ACCESSIBLE: Yes
EQUIPMENT NEEDED: Binoculars, walking shoes
COST: Free

ACCESSIBLE BY PUBLIC TRANSPORTATION: No
DISTANCE FROM DOWNTOWN PORTLAND: Twelve miles
FACILITIES: Restrooms, picnic shelter, canoe launch
SPECIAL COMMENTS: No bikes or motorized vehicles are allowed in the wetlands.

51 SMELL THE FLOWERS AT PENINSULA PARK ROSE GARDEN

Portland's oldest public rose garden literally keeps a low profile. The sunken English-style garden isn't visible from the street, so many Portlanders don't even know about this huge, lush North Portland garden. The more famous rose garden in Washington Park is often mobbed by tourists, but here you're more likely to find neighborhood kids splashing in the fountain, day-camp field trips, and a happy legion of volunteer pruners who consider their work a pleasure and a labor of love. Frederick Law Olmsted, who designed New York's Central Park, also designed Peninsula Park, which was established in 1903. The rose garden was added in 1914 as a mirrored garden, meaning each quarter mirrors the opposite quarter. Gardeners replanted the garden with new disease-resistant roses just before its 2014 centennial, so the rows look fresh and healthy. In summer, when you walk across Peninsula Park and get your first glimpse of the roses in full bloom, you might gasp and stop in your tracks.

700 N Rosa Parks Way   503-823-2525

WHEN TO GO: Summer

HOURS: 5:00 a.m.–midnight

KID-FRIENDLY: Very

DOG-FRIENDLY: Yes

WHEELCHAIR ACCESSIBLE: Yes

EQUIPMENT NEEDED: Camera

COST: Free

ACCESSIBLE BY PUBLIC TRANSPORTATION: Yes

DISTANCE FROM DOWNTOWN PORTLAND: Four miles

FACILITIES: Restroom

SPECIAL COMMENTS: Bring your swimsuit if you want to take a dip in Peninsula Park's pool.

52 TAKE AN URBAN SAFARI AT THE OREGON ZOO

A toddler peers into an enclosure and shrieks, awed, "It's a bear!" If the animals aren't enough, the Oregon Zoo has hundreds of displays and activities aimed at educating and engaging people of all ages, but especially kids. Elephant Lands opened in 2015 with six acres of habitat, mud wallows, and an elephant-sized swimming pool, providing the pachyderms with hours of family fun. For nature on a smaller scale, the insect zoo features thumb-sized green tobacco hornworms and the terrifyingly furry, yet shy Brazilian black tarantula. The zoo has helped bring California condors back from the brink of extinction. Strong-stomached visitors can watch the huge birds—twenty pounds, nine-foot wingspans—feed on stillborn calves from a local dairy. The thirty-inch narrow-gauge Washington Park and Zoo Railway has been running since 1958. Train buffs can get their postcard stamps canceled at America's last remaining railroad post office. In summer, the zoo offers concerts. Listen for monkeys and African wild dogs howling along with the musicians.

4001 SW Canyon Rd.
oregonzoo.org

WHEN TO GO: Year-round

HOURS: Summer: 9:30 a.m. to 6:00 p.m.; otherwise, 9:30 a.m. to 4:00 p.m.

KID-FRIENDLY: Extremely

DOG-FRIENDLY: No

WHEELCHAIR ACCESSIBLE: Yes

EQUIPMENT NEEDED: Comfortable shoes, camera

COST: Mar. 1–Sept. 30: adults, $14.95; seniors/military, $12.95; children, three to eleven, $9.95. Oct. 1–Feb. 28, adults, $9.95; seniors/military, $7.95; children three to eleven, $4.95

ACCESSIBLE BY PUBLIC TRANSPORTATION: Yes

DISTANCE FROM DOWNTOWN PORTLAND: Three miles

FACILITIES: Restrooms, restaurants, gift shop

SPECIAL COMMENTS: Plenty of indoor exhibits allow visitors to hide from the rain on dreary days.

53 EXPERIENCE PORTLAND HISTORY AT THE INTERNATIONAL ROSE TEST GARDEN

On the surface, the International Rose Test Garden in Washington Park is a place to stroll through rows of roses of every color and type, leaning in to give each a good sniff. Lean a little closer and you're looking deep into Rose City history. Jesse A. Currey founded the test garden in 1917 to protect European-grown hybrids from bombing during World War I. Currey was part of the Royal Rosarians, Portland's official goodwill ambassadors and Rose Festival promoters, known for their white suits and straw hats. A Rosarian statue welcomes visitors to the garden, and a walkway commemorates each Rosarian prime minister with an individual tile. The Rose Festival Queens Walk salutes the young ladies who presided over the festival, starting with Queen Flora in 1907. In one corner, the Shakespeare Garden contains plants mentioned in the playwright's works, and a bust of the Bard himself. The Shakespeare Garden is a favorite wedding spot. Nowadays, this is one of eleven test gardens in the US that determine which roses grow best in each part of the country, but most visitors rely on the sniff test to determine their favorites.

400 SW Kingston Ave.
503-823-3636

WHEN TO GO: May through September

HOURS: 7:30 a.m. to 9:00 p.m.

KID-FRIENDLY: Yes

DOG-FRIENDLY: Yes

WHEELCHAIR ACCESSIBLE: Partially

EQUIPMENT NEEDED: Camera

COST: Free

ACCESSIBLE BY PUBLIC TRANSPORTATION: Yes

DISTANCE FROM DOWNTOWN PORTLAND: Two miles

FACILITIES: Restroom, snack cart, gift shop

SPECIAL COMMENTS: On a clear day, this is a good place to come year-round for downtown and Mount Hood views.

54 LEARN ABOUT PLANTS AT THE LEACH BOTANICAL GARDEN

Surrounded by forest, Lilla and John Leach's 1930s stone cottage on Johnson Creek looks straight out of a fairy tale; in fact, it appeared in the cop/fantasy show *Grimm*. John's career as a pharmacist financed Lilla's passion for botany. The Klamath-Siskiyou region of southwest Oregon and northwest California fascinated her most, because heavy metals in the soil, hot summers, and wet winters supported plants that grew nowhere else. It was there that Lilla discovered her most important species, a pink shrub named *Kalmiopsis leachiana*. Today, the city owns the Leach property, which features a fern collection, rock garden, and plants that thrive in the shade—65 percent of the property is shaded, thanks to the extensive variety of trees. A winter interest trail focuses on leaf color, unusual bark, and fruits that stay on branches through the cold season. It's hidden in a far southeastern corner of the city, and on a warm day visitors can find solitude under a large hawthorn tree, listening to thousands of buzzing pollinators.

6704 SE 122nd Ave.
503-823-9503
leachgarden.org

WHEN TO GO: Year-round

HOURS: Tuesday–Saturday, 9:00 a.m. to 4:00 p.m.; Sunday 1:00 p.m. to 4:00 p.m.

KID-FRIENDLY: Yes, check out the Children's Garden, child-focused honeybee hikes, and scavenger hunt

DOG-FRIENDLY: No

WHEELCHAIR ACCESSIBLE: No

EQUIPMENT NEEDED: Walking shoes

COST: Free; donations encouraged

ACCESSIBLE BY PUBLIC TRANSPORTATION: Yes

DISTANCE FROM DOWNTOWN PORTLAND: Twelve miles

FACILITIES: Restrooms, gift shop, event space for weddings and memorials

SPECIAL COMMENTS: Good selection of books and pretty things in the gift shop

55 COUNT DOGS AT THE CORGI WALK IN THE PEARL DISTRICT

Every summer hundreds of Corgis and their people promenade through the Pearl District to raise money for the Oregon Humane Society and Corgi Rescue. Dog lover Lynde Paule founded the annual event in 2007, and it has grown steadily since that time. What these dogs lack in leg length they make up for with personality as they strut their stuff in costumes ranging from princess to convict. Every participant gets a special doggy scarf made by Corgi owner Barbara Kimberley. The 1.2-mile stroll meanders through the busy Pearl District, to the surprise and delight of unsuspecting bystanders who've never seen four hundred Corgis go on a walk together. The walk culminates in a massive Corgi takeover of the Jamison fountain, resulting in wet dogs galore. On 2017's tenth-anniversary walk, highlights included a fashion show and doggy ice cream social featuring Frosty Paws ice cream. You don't need a Corgi to find this event entertaining.

Portland Corgi Meetup Group
portlandcorgi.com

WHEN TO GO: August

HOURS: 9:00 a.m. to noon

KID-FRIENDLY: Yes

DOG-FRIENDLY: Yes, especially for Corgis

WHEELCHAIR ACCESSIBLE: Yes

EQUIPMENT NEEDED: Corgi, leash, walking shoes

COST: $25 for the first Corgi, $15 for each additional; free to watch

ACCESSIBLE BY PUBLIC TRANSPORTATION: Yes

DISTANCE FROM DOWNTOWN PORTLAND: One mile

FACILITIES: Porta-potty, restaurants and shopping in Pearl District

SPECIAL COMMENTS: Don't be surprised if you suddenly want to adopt a Corgi after watching this cute parade.

HOYT ARBORETUM (page 64)

CLACKAMAS RIVER (page 5)

BIKETOWN (page 31)

PORTLAND SATURDAY MARKET (page 128)

GEOCACHING (page 145)

SPRINGWATER CORRIDOR (page 46)

FIRST THURSDAY (page 122)

BELKNAP HOT SPRINGS (page 12)

MOVIE IN THE PARK (page 135)

56 TAKE YOUR KITTY TO FIRST CATURDAY

Dog people routinely take Fido on outings, but on the first Saturday of summer months, intrepid felines venture into a local park with their owners on the other end of the leash. This volunteer-run effort to socialize cats is part of a national movement and requires a bit of searching on Facebook to turn up the correct park for the month. As stated on the First Caturday website, "Many cats are fat and bored! Taking 'em outside to the park stimulates their maniacal brains." Cats are more suspicious than dogs, so First Caturday is less rambunctious than the dog park. A few cats play or climb trees (while leashed), many sit on their owners or lounge in the grass, and a few hiss or attempt to hide. Meanwhile, humans circulate, exclaiming over kitty cuteness. The ultimate goal? According to the website, "Some researchers speculate that once the global feline consciousness has been re-instated, wars across the lands will cease and a blissful peace will erupt, here on Earth."

facebook.com/firstcaturday

WHEN TO GO: First Saturdays during summer months; kitties don't like rain

HOURS: 1:30 p.m. to 4:30 p.m.

KID-FRIENDLY: Yes

DOG-FRIENDLY: Uh, no

WHEELCHAIR ACCESSIBLE: Usually

EQUIPMENT NEEDED: Cat, halter, leash, cat carrier; or cat appreciation

COST: Free

ACCESSIBLE BY PUBLIC TRANSPORTATION: Yes

DISTANCE FROM DOWNTOWN PORTLAND: Varies

FACILITIES: Varies

SPECIAL COMMENTS: Bring catnip to make more friends.

57 LEARN ABOUT ALPACAS

Jennifer Cameron was a full-time homemaker when her fifteen-year-old son told her to get a life. Two weeks later she attended an alpaca show at Portland's Expo Center. She was hooked. She unofficially interned with a veterinarian who specialized in alpacas and began to acquire her own herd. Now, more than a decade later, she and her husband, Bill, own an alpaca farm southeast of Portland with more than seventy alpacas. Visitors tour the huge barn, where they learn about herd behavior, gender differences and mating, and how alpaca fiber is harvested, sorted, and judged. Feeding time is the highlight of the tour. Visitors sit in folding chairs, quietly holding bowls of kibble. Jennifer releases the alpacas, and they trot over, heads bobbing, long necks reaching over each other seeking the best bowl, their adorable wooly faces right in your lap. Animal lovers will swoon. The farm offers special events, such as yoga with the alpacas in summer and occasional art nights.

Alpacas at Marquam Hill Ranch, 35835 OR-213, Molalla
503-407-3699   mhralpacas.com

WHEN TO GO: Year-round

HOURS: 10:00 a.m. to 4:00 p.m.

KID-FRIENDLY: Yes

DOG-FRIENDLY: No; they upset the alpacas. Please leave them at home.

WHEELCHAIR ACCESSIBLE: Yes

EQUIPMENT NEEDED: Camera

COST: $16 for the tour, free to visit ranch store

ACCESSIBLE BY PUBLIC TRANSPORTATION: No

DISTANCE FROM DOWNTOWN PORTLAND: Thirty-six miles

FACILITIES: Porta-potties, gift store

SPECIAL COMMENTS: Allow time for shopping. The store has everything from high-end sweaters to alpaca-shaped cookie cutters.

58 STUN YOUR EYEBALLS AT THE WOODEN SHOE TULIP FESTIVAL

Damp, chilly winter days in the Pacific Northwest lead to magnificent tulips in spring. Every year Wooden Shoe Tulip Farm in the agricultural region south of Portland celebrates with a tulip festival. The farm, owned by the Iverson family, began in 1950 and started growing tulips in 1974. By the 1980s, the family was selling bulbs, and in 1985 they decided to invite the public into their tulip fields during Easter weekend. A festival was born. This family-friendly event features a train ride through the tulips, wooden-shoe-making demonstrations, pony rides, a bouncy tent, and a market where you can buy potted tulips or preorder bulbs for fall. Visitors come to the annual Muddy Paws Fun Run/Walk—a benefit for Northwest Boxer Rescue—to run a 3K or 5K through the blooming fields with their dogs, but the big treat is being surrounded by forty acres of tulips in eye-zapping colors against the backdrop of white, pointy Mount Hood. Nature can't get much prettier than this.

33814 S Meridian Rd., Woodburn
503-634-2243   woodenshoe.com/events/tulip-fest

WHEN TO GO: Late March through early May

HOURS: 9:00 a.m. to 6:00 p.m.

KID-FRIENDLY: Yes

DOG-FRIENDLY: Yes

WHEELCHAIR ACCESSIBLE: The tulip fields can be uneven, but some areas of the festival are accessible.

EQUIPMENT NEEDED: Shoes for uneven ground, camera

COST: $5 age thirteen and up; maximum $20 per car

ACCESSIBLE BY PUBLIC TRANSPORTATION: No

DISTANCE FROM DOWNTOWN PORTLAND: Thirty-five miles

FACILITIES: Restrooms, food, wine tasting

SPECIAL COMMENTS: Serious about your photos? Buy a photographer's pass for $20 to get in early before the crowds.

59 CONTEMPLATE AT THE GROTTO

Ambrose Mayer built the original Catholic shrine—an altar cave carved into a 110-foot basalt cliff—in 1924 to fulfill a childhood promise to God after his mother almost died giving birth to his little sister. What was once designed as a place of religious contemplation on the outskirts of Portland is now surrounded by the city, but this shrine still retains an otherworldly quality, especially if you take the old elevator up the cliff and stroll the gardens. You don't have to be Catholic to feel peace sitting in the glass-walled meditation chapel with eastward views of snow-topped Mount Hood or ambling through the labyrinth. From late November through December, a million tiny lights festoon the Grotto's trees. "Silent Night" and other holiday favorites ring through the chilly, damp air as more than 150 choirs from around the state perform. For many Portlanders, warming their hands on a cup of hot chocolate while smelling hay from the petting zoo revives Christmas wonder.

8840 NE Skidmore St.
503-254-7371   thegrotto.org

WHEN TO GO: Open year-round; Festival of Lights runs from late November through December

HOURS: Opens at 9:00 a.m. Closing time varies by season.

KID-FRIENDLY: Yes

DOG-FRIENDLY: No

WHEELCHAIR ACCESSIBLE: Yes

COST: Free to visit main shrine, $6 to ride elevator to upper level

ACCESSIBLE BY PUBLIC TRANSPORTATION: Yes

DISTANCE FROM DOWNTOWN PORTLAND: Seven miles

FACILITIES: Restrooms, snacks, gift shop

SPECIAL COMMENTS: On summer Sundays, the Grotto celebrates the noon mass outside.

60 APPRECIATE BEAUTY AT LAN SU CHINESE GARDEN

Sixty-five artisans from Portland's sister city of Suzhou spent months assembling the traditional features of a Chinese garden. It's all here: water, stone, plants, architectural elements, and literary inscriptions. Hand-laid stone mosaics cover the ground, their patterns varying in different parts of the garden. A docent describes the garden's roughly two dozen Lake Tai sandstones, each sculpted differently by the waves of Lake Tai, as "frozen clouds." The garden changes with the season. On a summer evening, it's a tranquil respite from downtown, with waterfall sounds and the fragrance of jasmine and gardenia. Winter rains make the stonework glisten and the hefty koi happy. Lan Su is typical of a wealthy gentleman scholar's garden, whose erudite friends would drink tea and riff off the inscriptions—Taoist sayings and first lines of famous Chinese poems—all afternoon. The dark wood buildings are full of art, antique furniture, and calligraphy displays, and the tea house is exquisite in both menu and design.

239 NW Everett St.
503-228-8131
lansugarden.org

WHEN TO GO: Year-round

HOURS: Mar. 15–Oct. 31, 10:00 a.m. to 7:00 p.m.; Nov. 1–Mar. 14, 10:00 a.m. to 4:00 p.m.

KID-FRIENDLY: Only with close supervision

DOG-FRIENDLY: No

WHEELCHAIR ACCESSIBLE: Yes

EQUIPMENT NEEDED: Camera

COST: $10 adults, $9 seniors over sixty-two, $7 students six to eighteen or college students with ID, under five free

ACCESSIBLE BY PUBLIC TRANSPORTATION: Yes

DISTANCE FROM DOWNTOWN PORTLAND: One mile

FACILITIES: Restrooms, gift shop, teahouse

SPECIAL COMMENTS: The one-hour tour is highly recommended. Check out the online event calendar and you can time your visit to join a tai chi class, hear Chinese music, or watch a calligraphy demo for no extra charge.

61 PERFECT YOUR DOWNWARD GOAT

In spring 2016, Goat Yoga founder Lainey Morse was diagnosed with an autoimmune disease while going through a divorce. Only her pet goats brought her solace. She decided to share these therapeutic benefits with others, and soon Goat Yoga was born. The goats now travel several days a week for public classes at the Hanson Country Inn in Corvallis and Emerson Vineyards in Monmouth. Participants lay their mats on bumpy straw and pose while goats climb on their backs, chew on their hair, and do all the things goats do that would be inappropriate in an average yoga studio. The class is more focused on the joy of interacting with goats than perfecting a yoga pose, with many participants abandoning a downward dog to pet a wandering goat or take a selfie. Depending on the venue, yogis might be under a canvas tent to shelter from the rain or in the open air. Either way, the agricultural views of the Willamette Valley enhance the pastoral experience.

541-497-2149
goatyoga.net

WHEN TO GO: Warmer months for now; may be a year-round indoor location soon

HOURS: Classes are in the afternoons.

KID-FRIENDLY: Thirteen and up for regular classes, but watch the calendar for special children's goat yoga classes.

DOG-FRIENDLY: No

WHEELCHAIR ACCESSIBLE: No

EQUIPMENT NEEDED: Shoes you don't mind getting messy

COST: $35; $75 for goat yoga and wine tasting

ACCESSIBLE BY PUBLIC TRANSPORTATION: Yes

DISTANCE FROM DOWNTOWN PORTLAND: Eighty-six miles

FACILITIES: Restroom

SPECIAL COMMENTS: Plan to leave most of your possessions in the car, as goats nibble and pee.

62 DISCOVER PORTLAND'S HERITAGE TREES

In 1993, the Portland City Council enacted an ordinance to protect and celebrate historic trees. These heritage trees are important to the city because of their size, age, type, horticultural value, or historical association. Just over half of the designated trees are on private property. The rest are owned by the city. Designated heritage trees are protected from removal, and even pruning them requires special permission from the city forester. Almost three hundred heritage trees are currently alive and well in Portland, with the heaviest concentrations in the southeast and northeast. Many heritage trees are nonnative, such as Caucasian wingnuts, which are more at home in Azerbaijan, or Chilean monkey puzzles. Print a map of heritage trees from the Portland city website and take a self-guided tour. You'll know you've found the tree when you spy a small plaque on its trunk, usually facing the sidewalk. Stop, put your palm on the tree, close your eyes, and feel more than one hundred years of history in that bark.

Heritage tree map: portlandoregon.gov/parks/41049

WHEN TO GO: Year-round

HOURS: Daylight

KID-FRIENDLY: Yes

DOG-FRIENDLY: Yes

WHEELCHAIR ACCESSIBLE: Yes

EQUIPMENT NEEDED: Heritage tree map

COST: Free

ACCESSIBLE BY PUBLIC TRANSPORTATION: Varies, mostly

DISTANCE FROM DOWNTOWN PORTLAND: Varies

FACILITIES: None

SPECIAL COMMENTS: Because many heritage trees are on private land, be ready to observe from a distance.

FOOD
AND
CULTURE

63 SNACK WITH FORKTOWN FOOD TOURS

Portland is known as a culinary destination. Residents and visitors alike enjoy eating their way through neighborhoods. For those with a limited amount of time or who choose to defer to the experts, the enthusiastic guides at Forktown Food Tours will eagerly guide them directly to some of the city's best food. A typical downtown tour includes a beet salad appetizer at Nel Centro, followed by a half mile of sightseeing en route to homemade rigatoni at Grassa, and then hot falafels at Wolf and Bear's food cart. For dessert, a chocolate tasting at Cacao comes with a lesson on chocolate making and the origins of cacao beans. By the time participants visit all six stops, they'll have walked at least a mile, learned about the city's food scene and history, and have full stomachs. Forktown also gives food tours of the artsy Mississippi District and the recent restaurant explosion on Division Street.

503-234-3663
forktownfoodtoursportland.com

WHEN TO GO: Fairer weather

HOURS: Two and a half to three hours in the afternoon. Tour times vary.

KID-FRIENDLY: Only if your child has a sophisticated palate

DOG-FRIENDLY: No

WHEELCHAIR ACCESSIBLE: Yes

EQUIPMENT NEEDED: Walking shoes and rain jacket, depending on the season

COST: $85

ACCESSIBLE BY PUBLIC TRANSPORTATION: Yes

DISTANCE FROM DOWNTOWN PORTLAND: Depends on the tour

FACILITIES: Restroom stops along the way

SPECIAL COMMENTS: With advance notice, some Forktown tours can accommodate vegetarian, vegan, and gluten-free diets, and substitute nonalcoholic drinks. Be sure to ask ahead!

64 GET SPOOKED IN OREGON CITY

Established as a lumber mill town in 1829, Oregon City was the first incorporated city west of the Rockies and later served as Oregon's territorial capital. Rocky Smith has collected so many ghost stories about his hometown that he now offers multiple ghost tours. The McLoughlin neighborhood tour starts at the 1843 Francis Ermatinger House, Oregon City's oldest dwelling and now inhabited by the ghosts of a little girl and a boat captain. As participants wind through twenty blocks of the town, Smith delves into darker moments of Oregon City's history, including a steamboat explosion, suicides, and the treatment of Native Americans. Smith exuberantly recounts stories of the city's past residents, especially those whose energy is still hanging around. Besides running Northwest Ghost Tours since 2006, Smith is a high school art teacher, two-term city commissioner, director of the Oregon Ghost Conference, and Oregon City's citizen of the year for 2013. Visitors couldn't ask for a more knowledgeable guide to Oregon City.

P. O. Box 1214, Oregon City
503-679-4464   nwghosttours.com

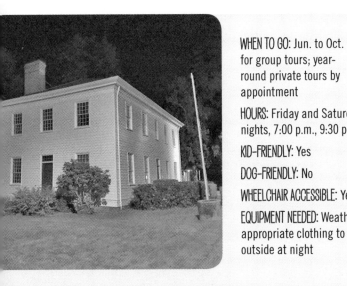

WHEN TO GO: Jun. to Oct. for group tours; year-round private tours by appointment

HOURS: Friday and Saturday nights, 7:00 p.m., 9:30 p.m.

KID-FRIENDLY: Yes

DOG-FRIENDLY: No

WHEELCHAIR ACCESSIBLE: Yes

EQUIPMENT NEEDED: Weather-appropriate clothing to be outside at night

COST: $15

ACCESSIBLE BY PUBLIC TRANSPORTATION: Yes

DISTANCE FROM DOWNTOWN PORTLAND: Thirteen miles

FACILITIES: None

SPECIAL COMMENTS: Rocky also offers tours of Oregon City art and murals, film locations, and history.

65 FINALLY UNDERSTAND SHAKESPEARE

Back in Shakespeare's day, theaters staged five to six plays every week. Hardworking actors had no time for rehearsing and memorizing their lines. Theater was faster paced, more interactive, and less formal than today's reverent Shakespeare productions. Portland's Original Practice Shakespeare Festival returns to these theatrical roots. Actors receive only their lines and cues—not the whole script—inspiring more reacting and improv. They learn between two and eight roles for each show so that the cast can constantly be shuffled, making each performance unique. OPS performs in Portland-area parks all summer, totaling more than thirty appearances. Audience members laze on the grass, sometimes at the actors' feet, and may find themselves involved in the action. An onstage prompter acts as host, cueing lines, troubleshooting, and keeping the story going. Sometimes the six-toed company cat, Sextus Augustus, attends. The actors—who are competitively paid professionals—wear modern clothes and carry tiny rolled-up scrolls with their lines. This is accessible theater, even for people who don't think they like Shakespeare.

503-479-5677
opsfest.org

WHEN TO GO: Summer

HOURS: Afternoon and evening performances

KID-FRIENDLY: Yes

DOG-FRIENDLY: Only for very patient, theater-loving canines

WHEELCHAIR ACCESSIBLE: Varies

EQUIPMENT NEEDED: Blanket or folding chair to sit on

COST: Free, but donations are appreciated

ACCESSIBLE BY PUBLIC TRANSPORTATION: Usually

DISTANCE FROM DOWNTOWN PORTLAND: Varies

FACILITIES: Varies

SPECIAL COMMENTS: Give it a try. This is much easier to understand than your typical Shakespeare play.

66 LEARN LOCAL HISTORY AT FORT VANCOUVER NATIONAL HISTORIC SITE

People visit Fort Vancouver both to ponder history and to walk or bike its vast green space. In 1829, British fur traders from the Hudson's Bay Company established this fort one hundred miles north of the Columbia River's mouth. Visitors can tour the reconstructed fort's fur store, counting house, and other buildings. The US Army built its first Northwest post here in 1849. The adjacent Pearson Air Museum chronicles the history of Pearson Field, one of the oldest American air fields still operating. Today, visitors can participate in events from different points in the fort's timeline, such as a 1950s swing dance at the air museum or an ethnobotany walk with a member of the Confederated Tribes of Grand Ronde—Native Americans were here before white settlers. The fort prides itself on its living history program. Indeed, you'll feel transported back to the 1830s as costumed rangers guide you through the shadow of the old wooden watch tower on a dark fall evening, your way lit only by lanterns.

612 E Reserve, Vancouver
360-816-6230
nps.gov/fova/index.htm

WHEN TO GO: Year-round

HOURS: Tuesday–Saturday, 9:00 a.m.–5:00 p.m.; park grounds daily, dawn to dusk

KID-FRIENDLY: Yes

DOG-FRIENDLY: Park grounds, yes. Fort, no. Check website for occasional Bark Ranger guided walking tours of the grounds.

WHEELCHAIR ACCESSIBLE: Yes

EQUIPMENT NEEDED: Walking shoes

COST: $5 to tour reconstructed fort, free for fifteen and under; free entrance to visitor center and Pearson Air Museum

ACCESSIBLE BY PUBLIC TRANSPORTATION: Yes

DISTANCE FROM DOWNTOWN PORTLAND: Nine miles

FACILITIES: Restrooms (only open during visitor center hours Tuesday–Saturday), gift shop

SPECIAL COMMENTS: Don't miss the fort's English garden, featuring plants the early settlers grew on-site.

67 TAKE A JAPANTOWN WALKING TOUR

Many Portland residents don't realize that the Chinatown/ Old Town neighborhood was once Japantown. Before the US government's unfortunate decision in 1942 to send Japanese-Americans to internment camps, this small section of Northwest Portland was home to Japanese-owned homes, hotels, restaurants, a bathhouse, and a judo studio. A free app called Japantown PDX maps out a walking tour for history buffs. Plug in your headphones and listen to snippets of stories about the Japanese experience in Portland while comparing 125 old photos to the current buildings. This is an adventure in history more than a workout, as you'll only cover about ten blocks. Standing in front of the old buildings where Japanese people lived and worked seventy years ago is much more tangible than reading a history book on your couch. The tour also covers others who settled in the area, especially Chinese and LGBT people. Bear in mind that this neighborhood is a bit seedy, so avoid ostentatiously flashing your smartphone.

itunes.apple.com/us/app/japantown-pdx/id806904198

WHEN TO GO: Year-round

HOURS: Daylight

KID-FRIENDLY: Yes

DOG-FRIENDLY: Yes

WHEELCHAIR ACCESSIBLE: Yes

EQUIPMENT NEEDED: iPhone, app

COST: Free

ACCESSIBLE BY PUBLIC TRANSPORTATION: Yes

DISTANCE FROM DOWNTOWN PORTLAND:
Downtown

FACILITIES: None

SPECIAL COMMENTS: Stop in at the Oregon
Nikkei Legacy Center to see museum
exhibits about the Japanese in Portland.

68 SEE CHERRIES BLOOM AT THE JAPANESE AMERICAN HISTORICAL PLAZA

In springtime, breezes loosen pink showers of cherry blossoms over picnickers and the hundreds of people taking portraits of loved ones under the blooming trees. This sweet family activity has dark roots: As a child, the future Japanese landscape architect Robert Murase was incarcerated in an internment camp near Topaz, Utah, in 1942. In 1990, after three years of fund-raising, his Japanese American Historical Plaza was dedicated to the 120,000 Japanese imprisoned during World War II. The plaza stretches between the Burnside Bridge and the Steel Bridge in Waterfront Park. When the cherry trees aren't blooming, most people jog or stroll past this part of the waterfront without noticing the poems etched into the plaza's carefully arranged boulders. Some capture the internment experience: "Black smoke roils. / Across the blue sky. / Winter chills our bones. / This is Minidoka." Others bravely look forward: "With new hope. / We build new lives. / Why complain when it rains? / This is what it means to be free."

West Waterfront

WHEN TO GO: Any time, but spring if you want to see the cherries in bloom

HOURS: 5:00 a.m. to midnight

KID-FRIENDLY: Yes

DOG-FRIENDLY: Yes

WHEELCHAIR ACCESSIBLE: Yes

EQUIPMENT NEEDED: Camera for cherry blossom photos

COST: Free

ACCESSIBLE BY PUBLIC TRANSPORTATION: Yes

DISTANCE FROM DOWNTOWN PORTLAND: One mile

FACILITIES: None

SPECIAL COMMENTS: Take your time and read the poems.

69 WALK THROUGH PORTLAND'S OLD JEWISH NEIGHBORHOOD

German Jews started coming to Oregon in the 1850s. Congregation Beth Israel formed in 1858, the year before Oregon's statehood. A wave of Russian Jews hit Oregon around the turn of the twentieth century, diversifying Portland's large Jewish population. The Oregon Jewish Museum and Center for Holocaust Education offers summer walking tours of the old Jewish neighborhood in South Portland. Walkers visit a settlement house, which was built to help immigrants adjust to life in America; the former library where many immigrants improved their English skills; an old synagogue; and the former site of Sarah Neusihin's pickle-making operation. Along the way, guides tell stories about Jewish Portland, informed by the museum's extensive oral history collection, and mention core Jewish values, such as *tzedakah*, or charitable giving. They evenhandedly discuss what was lost and gained by the old immigrant neighborhood making way for Highway 405 and downtown high-rises. The two-hour tour covers about 1.5 miles of easy walking and unearths a part of Portland's history that has mostly been buried beneath new development.

724 NW Davis St.
503-226-3600
ojmche.org

WHEN TO GO: Summer, check website for current dates

HOURS: Evening

KID-FRIENDLY: Not geared toward children

DOG-FRIENDLY: No

WHEELCHAIR ACCESSIBLE: Yes, but expect hills

EQUIPMENT NEEDED: Walking shoes

COST: $5

ACCESSIBLE BY PUBLIC TRANSPORTATION: Yes

DISTANCE FROM DOWNTOWN PORTLAND: Two miles

FACILITIES: None

SPECIAL COMMENTS: Everybody welcome, Jews and non-Jews

70 TASTE A BAZILLION APPLES

October heralds the beginning of cold temperatures and a long, gray season. One consolation: apples. Over two weekends every October, an apple-hungry mob descends on Portland Nursery. About fifty thousand people come to taste apples, listen to bands, decorate pumpkins in the Kids' Tent, drink apple cider, and generally welcome autumn. Staff members cut up thousands of apples per day for the massive apple tasting, and participants get checklists with tiny pencils to keep track of their reactions. They sample well-known varieties, such as Gala and Honeycrisp, and more obscure types, such as Northern Spy, Ashmead's Kernel, and Winter Banana. This is a rare opportunity to try unusual apples and then take home favorites for only 99 cents a pound. One section of the nursery turns into Scarecrow Alley for a creative scarecrow-building contest. Past entries have included a Day of the Dead-style mermaid, a giant crow, and a huge, veiny eyeball. The apple-tasting event, dating back to 1987, is a family tradition for many Portlanders.

5050 SE Stark St.
503-231-5050   portlandnursery.com

WHEN TO GO: Two weekends in October

HOURS: 10:00 a.m. to 5:00 p.m.

KID-FRIENDLY: Yes

DOG-FRIENDLY: No

WHEELCHAIR ACCESSIBLE: Yes

EQUIPMENT NEEDED: A hunger for apples

COST: Free

ACCESSIBLE BY PUBLIC TRANSPORTATION: Yes

DISTANCE FROM DOWNTOWN PORTLAND: Four miles

FACILITIES: Restrooms

SPECIAL COMMENTS: This is a beautiful nursery to wander through any day of the year.

71 EAT AT PORTLAND'S FAMOUS FOOD CARTS

Food carts are a phenomenon all around the US, but they're an institution in Portland. By 2001, the city already had 175 food carts; today, that number hovers around 500. Almost every neighborhood has its own cart pod, a long-term location where food entrepreneurs rent space to set up shop. Some pods have alluring amenities, such as porta-potties and covered—even heated—dining areas. Others, especially downtown, cater to those who plan to take lunch back to the office. Start-up costs are much lower than for traditional restaurants, so innovators gamble on niche concepts, such as vegan sushi, robot-made mini doughnuts, and Hawaiian barbecue. Some catch on, while others disappear within months. Cart pods are ideal for a group of people who want to eat different things together: for example, when you go out to lunch with your vegan sister, your gluten-free cousin, and your aunt with the tomato allergy. Because many offer shared seating, carts are a good way for locals and visitors to mix.

Food cart map: foodcartsportland.com/maps

WHEN TO GO: Year-round

HOURS: Varies

KID-FRIENDLY: Yes

DOG-FRIENDLY: Varies

WHEELCHAIR ACCESSIBLE: Yes

EQUIPMENT NEEDED: Appetite

COST: Most meals under $10

ACCESSIBLE BY PUBLIC TRANSPORTATION: Yes

DISTANCE FROM DOWNTOWN PORTLAND: Varies

FACILITIES: Varies

SPECIAL COMMENTS: Late-night eaters will appreciate Hawthorne Boulevard's Cartopia, which stays open until 4:00 a.m.

72 MEET LOCAL ARTISTS AT THE URBAN ART NETWORK FIRST THURSDAY ART WALK

At the beginning of the millennium, artists excluded from snooty galleries decided to show their art in the streets. Now, every first Thursday from April to November, while the Pearl District's upscale galleries host openings, dozens of talented artists set up their work along NW Thirteenth Avenue. Attendance at the street gallery varies according to the weather. If it's a blustery night, tarps and artwork may blow down the street, but you'll have a chance for long conversations with the artists. In fine weather, thousands of locals and visitors stream through, checking out the art and each other. The nonprofit, volunteer-run Urban Art Network accepts only artists who vend handmade products, such as painters, woodworkers, jewelers, clothing makers, and photographers. Anybody who wants to know the artist and the story behind a piece of artwork will enjoy this art-shopping experience. The lively and colorful street gallery will also inspire would-be artists.

NW 13th Avenue between Hoyt to Kearney
urbanartnetwork.org

WHEN TO GO: First Thursday, Apr. through Nov.

HOURS: 5:00 p.m. to 10:00 p.m.

KID-FRIENDLY: Yes

DOG-FRIENDLY: Dogs allowed but not encouraged

WHEELCHAIR ACCESSIBLE: Yes

EQUIPMENT NEEDED: None

COST: Free, but bring some money for artwork

ACCESSIBLE BY PUBLIC TRANSPORTATION: Yes

DISTANCE FROM DOWNTOWN PORTLAND: One-half mile

FACILITIES: Porta-potty

SPECIAL COMMENTS: Rain-or-shine event

73 GET WILD AT LAST THURSDAY

This monthly street fair singlehandedly helps "keep Portland weird," as the bumper sticker puts it. Locals and visitors wander artsy Northeast Alberta Street—or try to. The street is often so thick with artists, stilt walkers, fire dancers, drum circles, hula hoopers, and food vendors that pedestrians can hardly move. The event started in 1997, when boarded-up buildings lined Alberta and the neighborhood was better known for drive-by shootings than art. Artists living in the area started opening their low-rent studio/dwellings on the last Thursday of each month. This grass-roots movement slowly snowballed into the major street party it is today, with up to eighteen thousand people wandering Alberta Street on warm summer Thursdays. In June, July, and August, Alberta is closed to cars from Fifteenth to Thirtieth Avenues. Last Thursday has been controversial for years, as it sometimes gets too boisterous for neighborhood residents and business owners, but if you don't mind crowds this is a top opportunity for Portland people-watching and snagging unusual art finds.

NE Alberta Street between Fifteenth and Thirtieth

WHEN TO GO: Last Thursday of every month

HOURS: 6:00 p.m. to 9:00 p.m.

KID-FRIENDLY: Mostly

DOG-FRIENDLY: Might get trampled

WHEELCHAIR ACCESSIBLE: Proceed with caution

EQUIPMENT NEEDED: Comfortable shoes and cash

COST: Free

ACCESSIBLE BY PUBLIC TRANSPORTATION: Yes

DISTANCE FROM DOWNTOWN PORTLAND: Five miles

FACILITIES: Restaurants, boutiques, art

SPECIAL COMMENTS: If possible, bike, walk, or use public transportation, as parking is tight.

Visitors quickly learn about Portland's reputation for roses, bridges, bikes, and beer, but those interested in the Rose City's underbelly will love Portland Walking Tours' Underground Tour. It's nicknamed "the worst of Portland" and promises unsavory activities and bad behavior. Walkers meet at the company's Old Town office inside the historic Merchant Hotel and then meander through the neighborhood and down to the river. Stories focus on life in the nascent port city, when men outnumbered women fifteen to one, and newcomers risked being tricked into signing four-year contracts and being delivered— often unconscious—to unscrupulous boat captains. Most of the early female inhabitants were licensed "seamstresses"—their legal cover for prostitution. Gambling, the KKK, African American exclusion laws, Japanese internment during World War II, and organized crime are also covered. The tour ends back at the office, where participants descend to the basement, a former opium den. If this description makes you want to take a bath, choose the Best of Portland tour instead.

131 NW Second Ave.
503-774-4522 portlandwalkingtours.com

WHEN TO GO: Year-round

HOURS: Times and number of tours vary by season

KID-FRIENDLY: No

DOG-FRIENDLY: No

WHEELCHAIR ACCESSIBLE: No

EQUIPMENT NEEDED: Walking shoes

COST: $23

ACCESSIBLE BY PUBLIC TRANSPORTATION: Yes

DISTANCE FROM DOWNTOWN PORTLAND: Less than a mile

FACILITIES: Restroom in office

SPECIAL COMMENTS: The "Best of Portland" tour is ADA accessible and also welcomes dogs.

75 CELEBRATE SUMMER AT NEIGHBORHOOD STREET FAIRS

During the summer, when the sun finally shines, soggy, pasty Port-landers look for excuses to get outside. Neighborhood festivals offer the chance to spend an entire day shopping, eating, listening to bands, and talking to friends and neighbors in the streets of Port-land. From the Saint Johns Bizarre in May to the Belmont Street Fair in September, most major neighborhoods have their own festival. Each street fair aims to showcase what's special about their neigh-borhood. Good in the Hood, which has been running for a quarter century, features multicultural music and food in a traditionally African American part of Northeast Portland. The Lents Street Fair embraces the neighborhood's agricultural roots with a chicken beauty contest. All the street fairs are good places to buy jewelry, T-shirts, and artisan products directly from the makers and sample food from neighborhood restaurants. They're similar enough that you don't need to visit every single one, but in Portland, summer doesn't feel like summer without at least one street fair.

WHEN TO GO: May-September

HOURS: Varies, usually about 10:00 a.m. to 9:00 p.m.

KID-FRIENDLY: Yes

DOG-FRIENDLY: For superchill dogs

WHEELCHAIR ACCESSIBLE: Yes

EQUIPMENT NEEDED: Walking shoes, sunscreen, cash

COST: Free, but lots to buy

ACCESSIBLE BY PUBLIC TRANSPORTATION: Yes

DISTANCE FROM DOWNTOWN PORTLAND: Varies

FACILITIES: Porta-potties, food, shopping

SPECIAL COMMENTS: If possible, walk, bike, or take public transportation. The neighborhoods get crowded.

76 CULTIVATE SCOTTISH ROOTS AT THE PORTLAND HIGHLAND GAMES

When the mournful sound of bagpipes overtakes Mount Hood Community College and the athletic fields sport more tartan than workout wear, the Portland Highland Games is in session. Ever since 1952, Portland-area Scots and wannabe Scots have spent a day drumming, dancing, and practicing the extreme sports of their native land. Men and women throw very heavy things, be it a ninety-six-pound stone or a twenty-foot-long log called a caber. Visitors who prefer tunes to athletic grunting will enjoy highland dance competitions and Celtic musical acts. Hundreds gather to watch farmers and dogs attempt to herd wily sheep in what one spectator called "the age-old battle of man versus sheep." Clan tents sprinkle the edges of the field, helping festivalgoers trace their Scottish roots and thus select the proper tartan. This is the place for Portlanders to show off their kilts, shop for Celtic jewelry and velvet cloaks, and stock up on canned haggis.

26000 SE Stark St., Gresham
503-293-8501   phga.org

WHEN TO GO: One Saturday in July

HOURS: 8:00 a.m. to 6:00 p.m.

KID-FRIENDLY: Yes

DOG-FRIENDLY: No

WHEELCHAIR ACCESSIBLE: Yes

EQUIPMENT NEEDED: Money for snacks and souvenirs

COST: Adults, $20; youth six to seventeen, $10; under five, free

ACCESSIBLE BY PUBLIC TRANSPORTATION: Yes

DISTANCE FROM DOWNTOWN PORTLAND: Seventeen miles

FACILITIES: Restrooms, food, shopping

SPECIAL COMMENTS: You might get teased for wearing a floral-print scarf instead of tartan.

77 SHOP THE PORTLAND SATURDAY MARKET

Every weekend from March until Christmas Eve, Portland area artisans and vendors roll out their goods for Portland's biggest outdoor shopping experience. If you don't mind crowds, people-watching opportunities abound, and visitors get a feel for the diversity of locally produced goods. The market was founded in 1974, and a million people visit annually. White canvas vendor tents stretch from Naito Parkway to the Willamette River, bands set up in the street, and deep fryers exude the scent of Uruguayan empanadas, all adding up to a frenetic carnival feel. Meet the person who makes your arnica rub or lavender-scented dream pillow, ask artist Jessica Soleil why she draws an inspirational character called Super Pickle, and walk away with your feet newly hennaed. If you're shopping for Portland souvenirs for folks back home, you'll find personal and unusual gifts, each with a story straight from the artist's mouth. Locals rely on the Festival of the Last Minute for their Christmas shopping right up to Christmas Eve.

2 SW Naito Pkwy.
971-865-0382
portlandsaturdaymarket.com

WHEN TO GO: Saturdays and Sundays, March to December 24

HOURS: Saturdays, 10:00 a.m. to 5:00 p.m.; Sundays, 11:00 a.m. to 4:30 p.m.

KID-FRIENDLY: Very! Extra children's activities on the first Sunday of every month, July–October

DOG-FRIENDLY: Only for chill dogs

WHEELCHAIR ACCESSIBLE: Yes, but beware of crowds

EQUIPMENT NEEDED: Walking shoes and money

COST: Free, but you'll want spending money

ACCESSIBLE BY PUBLIC TRANSPORTATION: Yes

DISTANCE FROM DOWNTOWN PORTLAND: One mile

FACILITIES: Restrooms, food vendors

SPECIAL COMMENTS: A must for Portland people-watching

78 SOAK UP PORTLAND HISTORY AT LONE FIR CEMETERY

Portlanders established Mount Crawford Cemetery in 1855, renaming it Lone Fir in 1866. It's the resting place of many of the city's movers and shakers. Locals recognize the names on these tombstones from street signs around town. The park-like setting appeals to history buffs and botany aficionados. While Lone Fir started with the single eponymous fir, its collection of seven hundred mature trees is now second in size and scope only to the Hoyt Arboretum. Its rose garden contains descendants of roses brought to Oregon by pioneer women. The Firemen's Cemetery, established in 1862, is a special area deeded to firefighters. An active group of volunteers leads tours, organizes grave cleaning days, and puts on elaborate flashlight-led Halloween tours, featuring actors delivering monologues about the cemetery's historic inhabitants right on their graves. A walk through Lone Fir is an opportunity to soak up history, marvel at funerary art, remember the twenty-five thousand Portlanders buried here, and reflect on our own mortality.

SE Twenty-Sixth Avenue and Stark Street
503-797-1700
oregonmetro.gov/historic-cemeteries/lone-fir-cemetery

WHEN TO GO: Year-round

HOURS: Sunrise to sunset

KID-FRIENDLY: Not the top pick for most children

DOG-FRIENDLY: No

WHEELCHAIR ACCESSIBLE: Yes

EQUIPMENT NEEDED: None

COST: Free to look around, $10 donation for tours

ACCESSIBLE BY PUBLIC TRANSPORTATION: Yes

DISTANCE FROM DOWNTOWN PORTLAND: Two miles

FACILITIES: Porta-potty

SPECIAL COMMENTS: Choose from tours focusing on history or art and aesthetics.

79 REMEMBER OUR VETERANS AT THE OREGON VIETNAM VETERANS MEMORIAL

Five veterans and the parents of a fallen Marine envisioned a living memorial to the Vietnam War in Portland's Washington Park, and it was dedicated in 1987. Somber yet not depressing, this eight-acre war memorial garden is shaped like a basin. Visitors walk a memorial pathway along the rim, reading inscriptions on separate monuments that chronicle the names of lost soldiers and contemporary historical events. As the monument itself describes, "While the war raged in Vietnam, day to day life in Oregon continued. Recorded on these panels is a random selection of happenings—momentous and trivial, comic and tragic—which took place in towns and countryside from which the men named here had come and would not see again." These include anything from the 1966 Beach Bill deeming Oregon beaches public property to an Albany-born Playmate of the Year visiting troops. It really is a living memorial—visitors might even hear the eerie sounds of a bagpipe floating over the garden as a musician plays his individual tribute.

4000 SW Canyon Rd.
503-823-7529
portlandoregon.gov/parks/finder/index.
cfm?action=ViewPark&PropertyID=835

WHEN TO GO: Year-round

HOURS: 5:00 a.m. to 10:00 p.m.

KID-FRIENDLY: Not very

DOG-FRIENDLY: No

WHEELCHAIR ACCESSIBLE: Limited

EQUIPMENT NEEDED: Walking shoes, respect

COST: Free

ACCESSIBLE BY PUBLIC TRANSPORTATION: Yes

DISTANCE FROM DOWNTOWN PORTLAND: Three miles

FACILITIES: None

SPECIAL COMMENTS: No active sports, such as skateboarding or sledding, are allowed in the memorial area.

80 COMMUNE WITH SPIRITS ON A HAWTHORNE GHOST TOUR

On weekend nights, the Hawthorne Ghost Tour meanders up and down lively, hippie-ish Hawthorne Street, stopping to hear stories of spooks in the neighborhood and beyond. The two most haunted spots? The Bagdad Theatre, which opened in the days of vaudeville, and the Hawthorne Theatre. Why do ghosts like theaters so much? "I think it's the drama," says tour owner Marina Martinez. Neighborhood ghost stories include a peeping Tom who haunts a bathroom stall, a notorious killer whale trainer who now runs his spectral fingers through women's curly hair, and a woman-hating prostitute who still walks the streets. Martinez mixes history and hearsay, never letting facts interfere with a good story. None of the stories is too terrifying, and the slightly racy bits can be toned down for a family-friendly outing. Guests get two chances to communicate with spirits by holding a pair of dowsing rods and asking questions. When the spirits answer, things get a little eerie. Expect local jokesters to jump out of businesses and say, "Boo!"

714-675-1124   facebook.com/tourhawthorne

WHEN TO GO: Group tours, May to October. Private tours year-round by appointment.

HOURS: Friday and Saturday nights, 7:30 p.m. to 9:30 p.m.

KID-FRIENDLY: Yes

DOG-FRIENDLY: No

WHEELCHAIR ACCESSIBLE: Yes

EQUIPMENT NEEDED: Walking shoes, jacket, umbrella, depending on weather

COST: $20 adults; $10 children twelve and under

ACCESSIBLE BY PUBLIC TRANSPORTATION: Yes

DISTANCE FROM DOWNTOWN PORTLAND: Three miles

FACILITIES: Hawthorne Street has many restaurants, bars, and shops.

SPECIAL COMMENTS: Walking is minimal, but you should be comfortable standing for two hours.

81 WATCH A MOVIE IN A PARK

Admittedly, watching a movie while sprawled on a huge lawn may not be quite as comfortable as viewing one from your couch or a theater seat, but the novelty, fresh air, and community aspect of Portland's Movies in the Park have made it a popular annual event since 2007. Portlanders love to go outside in summer, when the rain finally abates, and lying under the stars with your family, friends, and neighbors on a mild July night is blissful. The evening usually starts with a local band as the crowd eagerly awaits nightfall, which comes around 8:00 or 9:00 during the summer. A popcorn vendor and a few food carts offer refreshments. Movies in the Park has grown to a twelve-week run, with about forty movies at forty different sites around the city. A typical season includes big Hollywood movies released in the last year, a few animated films, classics (think *Willy Wonka* or *Raiders of the Lost Ark*), and some indies.

503-823-7529
portlandoregon.gov/parks/69554

WHEN TO GO: Summer

HOURS: After sunset

KID-FRIENDLY: Very

DOG-FRIENDLY: For mellow canines who enjoy cinema

WHEELCHAIR ACCESSIBLE: Yes, for most sites

EQUIPMENT NEEDED: Blanket, jacket, snacks. People who bring chairs won't be loved by those behind them.

COST: Free, but bring cash for snacks

ACCESSIBLE BY PUBLIC TRANSPORTATION: Yes

DISTANCE FROM DOWNTOWN PORTLAND: Varies

FACILITIES: Restroom, food vendors

SPECIAL COMMENTS: You need to show up at least an hour early if you want a good spot.

FUN

AND

GAMES

82 CHASE THOSE FEBRUARY BLUES AWAY AT THE WINTER LIGHT FESTIVAL

By February, Portlanders feel the enervating effects of months of gray, rainy days. The Winter Light Festival is like light therapy for a whole city suffering from seasonal affective disorder. Started in 2016, this annual multiday event lures citizens away from Netflix and down to the waterfront with the promise of art installations, lit-up bridges, fire dancing, stilt walking, and free cruises on the *Portland Spirit*. The Oregon Museum of Science and Industry is at the heart of the event, offering talks on the scientific aspects of light and laser light shows in the planetarium. Everybody is welcome to join the illuminated bike ride or the lantern parade. Elaborate homemade lanterns in past parades have included a lit-up chicken piñata, a huge white owl, and festive yet practical light-festooned umbrellas. The Winter Light Festival reminds Portlanders that rain alone can't prevent them from eating a hot doughnut from a food cart while watching a fourteen-foot dragon sculpture spit fire.

pdxwlf.com

WHEN TO GO: February

HOURS: After dark

KID-FRIENDLY: Yes

DOG-FRIENDLY: Yes

WHEELCHAIR ACCESSIBLE: Yes

EQUIPMENT NEEDED: Light-up costumes encouraged; rain gear helps

COST: Free; donations appreciated

ACCESSIBLE BY PUBLIC TRANSPORTATION: Yes

DISTANCE FROM DOWNTOWN PORTLAND: One mile

FACILITIES: Restrooms, food carts

SPECIAL COMMENTS: Bundle up; it's February!

83 PLAY AT THE BEVERLY CLEARY SCULPTURE GARDEN

Fans of Beverly Cleary's classic children's series about Beezus and Ramona will delight in a darling sculpture garden tucked into Grant Park in Northeast Portland. Because most statues in the world depict serious adults, children are drawn to the bronze Ramona Quimby—looking carefree and wild in her rain jacket and rain boots—whether they've read Cleary's books or not. The bronze Henry Huggins looks like the dependable, clean-cut boy next door, while his dog, Ribsy, is crouched for play, a goofy grin on his face. Granite plaques denoting each of Cleary's books—from *Henry Huggins* in 1950 to *Ramona's World* in 1999—dot the paved area around the statues. The Newbery Medal-winning author was born thirty-eight miles away on a farm in McMinnville, Oregon. Her family moved to Northeast Portland when she started grade school. Cleary played in Grant Park as a child, and her characters live on nearby Klickitat Street. Children's literature fans will enjoy visiting the park and neighborhood to follow in Cleary's footsteps.

NE Thirty-Third Avenue and NE Brazee Street   503-823-2333

WHEN TO GO: Year-round

HOURS: Daylight

KID-FRIENDLY: Very

DOG-FRIENDLY: Don't pee on Ribsy

WHEELCHAIR ACCESSIBLE: Yes

EQUIPMENT NEEDED: None

COST: Free

ACCESSIBLE BY PUBLIC TRANSPORTATION: Yes

DISTANCE FROM DOWNTOWN PORTLAND: Four miles

FACILITIES: Restroom

SPECIAL COMMENTS: You might want to reread Cleary's books after visiting.

84 EXPERIENCE THE ROSE FESTIVAL

In 1907, city leaders debuted the annual Rose Festival as part of a marketing ploy to brand Portland the "summer capital of the world." More than a hundred years later, the branding strategy's failed, but the festival lives on. Events now stretch over a five-week period, attracting five million visitors from around the world. Top draws include the Starlight Parade, Grand Floral Parade, and CityFair. The Starlight Parade dates all the way back to the festival's first year—back then the night parade featured streetcars decorated with electric lights and the governor's daughter as Rose Queen. The Grand Floral Parade boasts floats covered with organic matter, such as flowers, roots, and seeds. In the US, only Pasadena has a larger floral parade. CityFair sets up on the waterfront for three consecutive weekends and includes carnival rides, visits from navy ships, and such special treats as deep-fried rose petals. Some Scrooge-like locals grumble about the festivities tying up traffic, but every Portlander should experience the Rose Fest parades at least once.

Rose Building, 1020 SW Naito Pkwy.
503-227-2681   rosefestival.org

WHEN TO GO: Late May/early June

HOURS: Varies by event

KID-FRIENDLY: Yes

DOG-FRIENDLY: Yes

WHEELCHAIR ACCESSIBLE: Yes

EQUIPMENT NEEDED: Tolerance for crowds

COST: CityFair costs $8; under seven, free

ACCESSIBLE BY PUBLIC TRANSPORTATION: Yes

DISTANCE FROM DOWNTOWN PORTLAND: Varies; most events downtown

FACILITIES: Porta-potties, restaurants

SPECIAL COMMENTS: Bring a rain jacket, as the floral parade seems to attract drizzle.

85 LIVE A FAIRY TALE AT THE ENCHANTED FOREST

Small children will feel like they're living in a fairy tale as they walk under a giant, drooping nose to enter a witch's mouth or crawl down a rabbit hole to look for Alice. Roger Tofte, a draftsman for the Oregon State Highway Department and father of four, began creating this magical land seven miles south of Salem in 1964. In 1971, the original Storybook Trail opened, allowing visitors to turn a bend in a forest path and stumble upon life-sized fairy tale tableaux. In the years since, Tofte has added a Western Town, Old European Village, haunted house, roller coaster, and children's rides. Visitors can stop in the European Village to hear Irish music or watch a performance of an updated fairy tale, such as *Snow White and the Seven Dorks,* in the comedy theater. This family-run theme park hearkens back to a time when kids wanted to hear a story more than play with Mom's phone, and it honors individual creations over the mass produced.

8462 Enchanted Way SE, Turner
503-371-4242
enchantedforest.com

WHEN TO GO: Open Mar.—Sept.; daily in summer and spring break, weekends only in spring and Sept.

HOURS: Opens 10:00 a.m.; depending on the day and month, closes between 4:00 p.m. and 7:00 p.m.

KID-FRIENDLY: Extremely

DOG-FRIENDLY: Service only

WHEELCHAIR ACCESSIBLE: Yes, but park is built on a hill. Wheelchair assistance provided upon request.

EQUIPMENT NEEDED: Comfortable shoes

COST: $12.50 adults; $10.95 children three to twelve and seniors; rides and some attractions cost extra

ACCESSIBLE BY PUBLIC TRANSPORTATION: No

DISTANCE FROM DOWNTOWN PORTLAND: Fifty-four miles

FACILITIES: Restaurants, restrooms, shopping

SPECIAL COMMENTS: One of the few theme parks where you can bring your own food.

86 PET A LLAMA AND EAT A FUNNEL CAKE AT THE CLARK COUNTY FAIR

Clark County, just over the border in Washington State, has enough wide-open agricultural space to produce a perfect fair. Ag displays include cows, horses, and vegetable-growing competitions. Local superstar Rojo is usually there, along with his gang of therapy alpacas and fellow llamas. Entertainment ranges from big-name rock bands of yore to monster truck rallies to high-jumping dock dogs splashing into a pool of water. No wonder a quarter million people attend annually. When you see the long ice-cream line at the Clark County Dairy Women booth or watch a child display her prize goat, you realize that farms and 4-H are alive and well just outside of hip Portland. As the sun goes down and the midway lights come on, walking under the shadow of the giant wheel or hearing music pound from the Gravitron may stir those feelings of excitement and possibility hidden away in your inner teenager.

17402 NE Delfel Rd., Ridgefield
360-397-6180   clarkcofair.com

WHEN TO GO: Early August, dates vary

HOURS: Sunday–Thursday, 10:00 a.m. to 10:00 p.m.; Friday and Saturday, 10:00 a.m. to 11:00 p.m.

KID-FRIENDLY: Yes

DOG-FRIENDLY: No

WHEELCHAIR ACCESSIBLE: Yes

EQUIPMENT NEEDED: Sneakers and sunscreen

COST: $11.25 adults; $9.25 seniors; $8.25 children seven to twelve; six and under free

ACCESSIBLE BY PUBLIC TRANSPORTATION: Yes

DISTANCE FROM DOWNTOWN PORTLAND: Seventeen miles

FACILITIES: Restrooms, funnel cakes, other fair fare

SPECIAL COMMENTS: Plan ahead and enter your best vegetable in the contest.

87 TRY GEOCACHING

In 2000, before everybody had GPS-enabled phones, geocaching started as a fringe hobby among tech professionals. The pastime has local roots: One of the earliest caches was hidden in the woods in nearby Beavercreek, Oregon. Nowadays, geocachers use their phones to search for treasure other players have hidden, be it a small toy or a logbook to sign to prove they found it. Newbies start by downloading a geocaching app that lists nearby caches with cute names, such as "L'il Pink Houses" or "Lightsaber," difficulty ratings for finding the cache and navigating terrain, and the size of the container. Sizes generally range from a film canister to a five-gallon bucket. Depending on what part of Portland they're in, geocaching newbies may be surprised to learn of a dozen caches within walking distance. Part of the fun is being in on the secret and stealthily finding caches without "muggles"—that is, non-geocachers—catching on. Geocaching is a great family activity where nobody gets yelled at for not putting down their phone.

geocaching.com

WHEN TO GO: Year-round

HOURS: Depends on the cache; those inside businesses are only accessible during business hours.

KID-FRIENDLY: Very

DOG-FRIENDLY: Varies

WHEELCHAIR ACCESSIBLE: Varies; the app gives details for each cache.

EQUIPMENT NEEDED: GPS-enabled phone

COST: Free, unless you want to upgrade to premium caches

ACCESSIBLE BY PUBLIC TRANSPORTATION: Varies

DISTANCE FROM DOWNTOWN PORTLAND: Varies

FACILITIES: None

SPECIAL COMMENTS: Be prepared to look a little shady when searching for treasures in heavily trafficked parts of town.

88 GO FLIGHTSEEING WITH ENVI ADVENTURES

Even lifelong residents of Portland will be surprised by how the city looks from above. Envi Adventures' four-seater plane flies out of Troutdale Airport, just east of Portland. The staff of the small tour company is excited to share aerial views of downtown Portland, the Columbia River Gorge, Mount Hood, and nearby waterfalls. Passengers arrive at the appointed time and wait for the little Cessna 182 to roll up. After boarding, the pilot hashes out the flight plan with air traffic control and distributes headsets for in-air communication. The little plane feels surprisingly like a car, with one passenger shoulder-to-shoulder with the pilot and the other two in the backseat. Flying over Portland's bridges at 120 miles per hour, checking out Ross Island and Willamette Falls from above, reveals hidden details of the city, giving passengers a new perspective on Portland. Envi offers seasonal specials, including flying over the Sauvie Island pumpkin patch and corn maze in autumn, Christmas lights in December, and sunset flights for Valentine's Day.

920 NW Perimeter Way, Troutdale
503-967-9622
enviadventures.com

WHEN TO GO: Year-round

HOURS: By appointment

KID-FRIENDLY: Yes

DOG-FRIENDLY: No

WHEELCHAIR ACCESSIBLE: No

EQUIPMENT NEEDED: Camera

COST: $99–$349 per flight (not per passenger)

ACCESSIBLE BY PUBLIC TRANSPORTATION: No

DISTANCE FROM DOWNTOWN PORTLAND: Eighteen miles

FACILITIES: Restroom, lounge at airport

SPECIAL COMMENTS: The per-flight pricing structure makes flightseeing surprisingly affordable when split three ways.

89 RIDE THE ROLLER COASTER AT OAKS AMUSEMENT PARK

The sounds of darts popping balloons, a rumbling roller coaster, and children shrieking with laughter liven up the east bank of the Willamette River in Portland's Sellwood neighborhood. The Coney Island of the Northwest, as it was called when it opened in 1905, is now one of the country's longest-running amusement parks. An old-fashioned fairway includes games, kiddie rides, and as many curly fries and corndogs as you can eat. Admission is free. Visitors can people-watch for an hour, spring for a round of mini golf, or buy a ride bracelet and make a day of it. When fireworks zing through the sky over the Willamette, Oaks Park offers a front-row view, making it a wildly popular Fourth of July destination. Roller skating is also big here—if the day turns rainy, visitors can join a skating session in the oldest rink west of the Mississippi. Or, watch the semipros battle it out in the Hangar, home to the Rose City Rollers roller derby league.

7805 SE Oaks Park Way
503-233-5777   oakspark.com

WHEN TO GO: Summer

HOURS: Check the website for special event closings.

KID-FRIENDLY: Yes

DOG-FRIENDLY: Yes

WHEELCHAIR ACCESSIBLE: Yes

EQUIPMENT NEEDED: Comfortable shoes

COST: Free admission, free parking. Prices of attractions vary. A deluxe ride bracelet costs $19.

ACCESSIBLE BY PUBLIC TRANSPORTATION: Yes

DISTANCE FROM DOWNTOWN PORTLAND: Five miles

FACILITIES: Burger joints, restrooms, games, rides

SPECIAL COMMENTS: Consider biking to Oaks; it's right on the Springwater Corridor.

90 GET LOST IN THE ORIGINAL CORN MAIZE ON SAUVIE ISLAND

When the dark nights lengthen and Portland takes a turn for the chilly, maze architects on Sauvie Island unveil their cornfield designs. The Original Maize at the Pumpkin Patch debuted in the late '90s. Since then, other corn mazes have opened on the island and in the Portland metro. These annual events generally feature a family-friendly atmosphere with all the harvest festival trimmings: pumpkins, hot cider, hay rides, and farm animals. Some mazes also feature haunted versions more appropriate for teenagers and others who enjoy getting spooked. The basic maze can be hard enough to solve on a dark, damp night, even without ghouls popping out of the twelve-foot corn—at least one parent has offered a worker a cash bribe to learn the quickest way out. There's a real art to building these mazes, but you can only see the design in aerial photos. The Original Corn Maize has depicted Lewis and Clark, the Trailblazers logo, and the popular heart inside the shape of Oregon.

16511 NW Gillihan Rd.
503-621-7110   portlandmaize.com

WHEN TO GO: Late September through Halloween

HOURS: 10:00 a.m. to 6:00 p.m.; Fridays and Saturdays in October, open until 10:00 p.m.

KID-FRIENDLY: Yes

DOG-FRIENDLY: Yes in maze and parking lot only. No in pumpkin patch and other areas.

WHEELCHAIR ACCESSIBLE: No

EQUIPMENT NEEDED: Rain boots or other sturdy walking shoes, jackets

COST: $8 for adults; $6 for seniors and children six to twelve; free for five and under

ACCESSIBLE BY PUBLIC TRANSPORTATION: No

DISTANCE FROM DOWNTOWN PORTLAND: Thirteen miles

FACILITIES: Restrooms, treats

SPECIAL COMMENTS: Prepare for mud.

91 TEST YOUR OBSTACLE COURSE SKILLS AT WEST COAST FITNESS' OUTDOOR TRAINING YARD

This family-owned gym has served the Saint Johns neighborhood since 1994. In addition to its enormous selection of weights, machines, and classes, West Coast boasts an outdoor obstacle course that owner Terri Chadney terms "an adult playground." She and her husband, Jay, spent two years building a strength-challenging mix of log vaults, monkey bars, a cargo net to climb, and a sand run with huge tires to pull or flip. The gym's personal trainers incorporate this equipment into group exercise classes, or people can use it on their own. Terri's inspiration was obstacle course proponent Pete Egoscue, founder of Patch Fitness. The Patch fundamentals are go over, under, and around something; challenge and remove your limitations; use many different environments; and have fun. The idea is for adults to interact with structures just as a child incorporates random stuff into play. Looking down on busy Lombard Street after climbing to the top of the cargo net or making it across the monkey bars gives a feeling of accomplishment and satisfaction the treadmill doesn't deliver.

7522 N Lombard St.
503-283-5404
pdxgym.com

WHEN TO GO: Daylight

HOURS: Gym is open Mon–Fri, 4:00 a.m. to 11:00 p.m.; Sat/Sun, 6:00 a.m. to 11:00 p.m.

KID-FRIENDLY: No

DOG-FRIENDLY: No

WHEELCHAIR ACCESSIBLE: No

EQUIPMENT NEEDED: Athletic shoes and workout wear

COST: Free to members; $20 drop-in includes full access to gym and classes

ACCESSIBLE BY PUBLIC TRANSPORTATION: Yes

DISTANCE FROM DOWNTOWN PORTLAND: Five miles

FACILITIES: Restrooms, showers, lockers

SPECIAL COMMENTS: Long pants will prevent rope burns from the cargo net.

92 CLIMB AND SWING AT HARPER'S PLAYGROUND

As Cody and April Goldberg's daughter, Harper, was growing up, they realized her physical challenges would prevent her from accessing Portland's playgrounds. So they decided to raise money and design the city's first inclusive playground. Using the motto "More play for more people," they gathered community donations ranging from $5 to $75,000. In 2012, Harper's Playground opened. It's designed to attract all children, regardless of physical ability, with adaptive swings, extrawide slides, a climbing net, and lots of benches for parental supervision and resting. The sandbox includes a water faucet so children can play in wet sand, just like at the beach. Designers planned for the whole park to be accessible without obvious wheelchair ramps so that everybody feels equal. Darling bronze sculptures of starfish, Hawksbill sea turtles, and other critters by artist Peter Helzer are integrated into the design. Many families from outside Portland come here to give their children an opportunity to play.

2525 N Dekum St.
503-823-2525
harpersplayground.org

WHEN TO GO: Year-round

HOURS: 5:00 a.m. to midnight

KID-FRIENDLY: Very

DOG-FRIENDLY: Yes

WHEELCHAIR ACCESSIBLE: Yes

EQUIPMENT NEEDED: Play clothes

COST: Free

ACCESSIBLE BY PUBLIC TRANSPORTATION: Yes

DISTANCE FROM DOWNTOWN PORTLAND: Six miles

FACILITIES: Restrooms, drinking fountains, picnic table

SPECIAL COMMENTS: Adults can play here too.

93 SPARK CHRISTMAS AWE AT PDX RACEWAY'S WINTER WONDERLAND

The Portland International Raceway occupies an area of North Portland near the Columbia River once called VanPort. This mostly African American neighborhood housed shipbuilders during World War II, soaring to a peak population of forty thousand before being destroyed in the massive flooding of 1948. The City of Portland acquired the land in 1960 and turned it into a race track. Nowadays, cars, motorcycles, and bikes zip around the 1.97-mile track, which hosts about 550 events a year. In December, the track gussies up for the holidays. Millions of Christmas lights illuminate bleak winter nights on the raceway. Lines of cars slowly snake through, so visitors can see the light displays from a warm car interior. Hardy souls park their cars and turn out for special event nights, such as Bike the Lights, and the Lights and Leashes Dog Walk. Brave the rain and check out lights forming traditional holiday subjects, such as reindeer, toy soldiers, stars, and the twelve days of Christmas.

1940 N Victory Blvd.
503-823-2176   winterwonderlandportland.com

WHEN TO GO: Late November through Christmas

HOURS: 5:30 p.m. to 9:30 p.m.

KID-FRIENDLY: Very

DOG-FRIENDLY: Yes

WHEELCHAIR ACCESSIBLE: Yes

EQUIPMENT NEEDED: Car, bike, dog, or sneakers, depending on the night

COST: Charge per type of vehicle, $20 for a regular car

ACCESSIBLE BY PUBLIC TRANSPORTATION: Yes

DISTANCE FROM DOWNTOWN PORTLAND: Seven miles

FACILITIES: Restroom

SPECIAL COMMENTS: It's December, so bring your rain gear.

94 CELEBRATE THE HOLIDAYS WITH ZOO LIGHTS

Every December, the wildly popular Zoo Lights fills the sixty-four-acre zoological park with 1.6 million light bulbs, formed on hand-welded metal frames in animal shapes. Displays range from beloved storybook animals, such as the farm animals of the Bremen Town Musicians from the Grimm fairy tale, to a 3-D secretary bird and giant African baobab trees to Christmas-specific leaping reindeer. Building these frames and zip-tying on lights is a year-round endeavor for the behind-the-scenes crew who create this magical holiday atmosphere, and every year the zoo outdoes itself by adding more lights and new displays. Ride the little zoo train for maximum dazzle. Besides massive holiday cheer, visitors might finally see those nocturnal animals that sleep through their daytime zoo trips—at least the animals brave or curious enough to venture into the bright lights.

4001 SW Canyon Rd.
oregonzoo.org/visit/zoolights

WHEN TO GO: Late November through December

HOURS: 5:00 p.m. to 9:00 p.m.

KID-FRIENDLY: Yes

DOG-FRIENDLY: No

WHEELCHAIR ACCESSIBLE: Yes

EQUIPMENT NEEDED: Warm clothes and walking shoes

COST: $14.95 for adults; $9.95 for children

ACCESSIBLE BY PUBLIC TRANSPORTATION: Yes. Highly recommended; the parking lot is a zoo!

DISTANCE FROM DOWNTOWN PORTLAND: Two miles

FACILITIES: Restrooms, food and drink

SPECIAL COMMENTS: Buy your tickets online and print them at home to save time. Ticket lines are long.

95 TAKE FIDO TO A DOG PARK

Because Portlanders love their dogs, many city parks have off-leash areas, but a few dog parks stand above the rest. Normandale Park in Northeast Portland is one of nine fenced dog parks in the city. A double gate system prevents dogs from bolting. Once through the gates, three separate fenced-off areas await—one reserved for dogs under twenty-five pounds and two for bigger dogs or those who run with the big dogs. Amenities include trees, water bowls, picnic tables, and downed logs that double as benches for humans and canine climbing toys. Wood chips prevent the park from getting muddy. On Portland's West Side, Gabriel Park's 1.5-acre, fenced off-leash area is a top draw for dogs and their people, though it's only open in the dry season, from May to October. Fenced dog parks are a fun way for dogs to socialize and exercise while owners chat, relax, and secretly revel in the fact that their dog is the cutest.

NE Fifty-Seveneth Avenue at Halsey Street
503-823-7529
portlandoregon.gov/parks/39523

WHEN TO GO: Year-round

HOURS: 5:00 a.m. to midnight

KID-FRIENDLY: Yes

DOG-FRIENDLY: Yes

WHEELCHAIR ACCESSIBLE: Yes

EQUIPMENT NEEDED: Dog, cleanup bags

COST: Free

ACCESSIBLE BY PUBLIC TRANSPORTATION: Yes

DISTANCE FROM DOWNTOWN PORTLAND: Five miles

FACILITIES: Restroom

SPECIAL COMMENTS: Watch your step. Please clean up after your dog.

96 PLAY HORSESHOES IN LAURELHURST PARK

In a time when most people expect the explosions and thrills of video games, an activity such as horseshoes moves at a glacial pace. But on a warm summer evening, consider the retro pleasures of hanging out in a park with a few friends and throwing horseshoes at a stake in the ground. Laurelhurst Park in Southeast Portland has a rare feature: a dedicated horseshoe court. Because this is mostly a game played by old-timers, the number of people showing up for the Wednesday night club has dwindled down to only a few. It's clearly time for a horseshoe revival. To play, you need a set of horseshoes—available online—and two people. Four people can make two teams of two. Players take turns throwing their horseshoes, trying to get a ringer by hitting the stake or landing their shoes as close to the stake as possible. People craving a simple, sociable outside activity and a break from screen time might enjoy this relaxing game.

SE Cesar Chavez Boulevard and Stark Street;
horseshoe court near the southeast corner of the park   503-823-2525

WHEN TO GO: Dry days are nicest.

HOURS: Daylight

KID-FRIENDLY: Yes

DOG-FRIENDLY: No

WHEELCHAIR ACCESSIBLE: No

EQUIPMENT NEEDED: Horseshoes, paper and pen for scoring

COST: Free

ACCESSIBLE BY PUBLIC TRANSPORTATION: Yes

DISTANCE FROM DOWNTOWN PORTLAND: Three miles

FACILITIES: Restroom

SPECIAL COMMENTS: If you're polite, maybe the old-timers will let you join their horseshoe club.

97 PRACTICE YOUR SWING AT A PUBLIC GOLF COURSE

Portland's five public golf courses are friendly and welcoming, even to newbies. If you haven't picked up golf clubs before, buy a bucket of balls and practice your swing on the driving range. *Golf Digest* ranks Southeast Portland's Eastmoreland one of the top public courses to play. There, golfers of all levels improve their form on the driving range—a huge grassy area marked with distances where players work independently on their swing. Players can also practice sinking the ball into a hole on the mini golf-sized putting green or work on chip shots on the chipping green. Newbies who don't know their driver from their seven iron can book private or small-group lessons. The public courses are an accessible way for the golf-curious to try the sport without snootiness or elitism, while getting fresh air and gentle exercise on sparkling green grass. Bonus: snacks and microbrews at the outdoor café and a full selection of plaid shorts and other classic golf attire in the pro shop.

2425 SE Bybee Blvd.
503-775-2900
eastmorelandgolfcourse.com

Public golf courses in Portland
portlandoregon.gov/parks/63560

WHEN TO GO: Year-round

HOURS: Varies by course, generally opening around 6:00 a.m.

KID-FRIENDLY: Mini golf might be better

DOG-FRIENDLY: No

WHEELCHAIR ACCESSIBLE: No

EQUIPMENT NEEDED: You can rent clubs from the course.

COST: Varies by season, time of day, and equipment needed. For example, at Eastmoreland, eighteen holes costs $42 on a summer weekend and $22 for a winter weekday.

ACCESSIBLE BY PUBLIC TRANSPORTATION: Yes

DISTANCE FROM DOWNTOWN PORTLAND: Varies by course

FACILITIES: Restrooms, café, pro shop

SPECIAL COMMENTS: If you're totally new, book a lesson or bring a friend who knows the game.

98 GO COSMIC TUBING AT MOUNT HOOD

Mount Hood offers the country's only chance to fly down a snowy slope on an inner tube, a laser light show illuminating your descent while music pulses. Visitors don't even have to drag their tubes back up the mountain to do it again. Instead, they board a moving walkway that serves as a tube lift. Sixty thousand LED lights and a DJ set this experience apart from ordinary sledding or tubing. Tubes come in single, double, and four-person models. The heavier the tube, the faster it goes, so pile on three of your friends or family members and you'll be grateful for the orange plastic fencing that guards tubers from going off a snowy drop at the bottom of the hill. Daredevils can try the Extreme Tube Hill (helmet recommended), while tiny tots can play on the Kiddie Tube Hill. A café on top of the hill provides an opportunity to warm up by a stone fireplace with a burger or an espresso.

87000 US 26, Government Camp
503-272-3206
skibowl.com

WHEN TO GO: Winter until early spring

HOURS: 5:00 p.m. to 10:00 p.m.

KID-FRIENDLY: Yes!

DOG-FRIENDLY: No

WHEELCHAIR ACCESSIBLE: No

EQUIPMENT NEEDED: Warm clothes

COST: $30/adults for two hours; $24/children for two hours

ACCESSIBLE BY PUBLIC TRANSPORTATION: No

DISTANCE FROM DOWNTOWN PORTLAND: Fifty-seven miles

FACILITIES: Restroom, café, first aid station

SPECIAL COMMENTS: Go after dark for maximum effect.

99 WATCH THE PORTLAND ADULT SOAPBOX DERBY

Every August since 1997, a crowd converges to watch soapbox racers zoom down Mount Tabor's steep slopes. Cars must have at least three wheels, brakes, and a horn. Some soapbox designers aim for speed, while others are all about creativity. Past entrants have included a giant dachshund and a beauty shop on wheels, complete with an old-fashioned hooded hair dryer and ladies in curlers. Up to ten thousand spectators line the long raceway, picnicking, drinking beer, and jumping out of the way whenever an official bellows, "Clear the course!" Except for this safety concern, it's a casual party atmosphere, with occasional long waits for the next set of racers to ready their cars for the descent. Teams race the course three times, and then come the championship rounds. Award categories include engineering, speed, and art. Spectators should bring extra sunscreen in case they get blasted by a soapbox-mounted super soaker.

SE Sixtieth Avenue and Salmon Street
soapboxracer.com

WHEN TO GO: Usually the third Saturday of August

HOURS: 9:30 a.m. to 4:00 p.m.-ish

KID-FRIENDLY: Yes

DOG-FRIENDLY: Yes

WHEELCHAIR ACCESSIBLE: Paved but steep

EQUIPMENT NEEDED: Sunscreen, hat, drinks, snacks

COST: Free

ACCESSIBLE BY PUBLIC TRANSPORTATION: Yes

DISTANCE FROM DOWNTOWN PORTLAND: Six miles

FACILITIES: Restrooms

SPECIAL COMMENTS: Beware, as many spectators get the bug to create a car for next year's derby.

100 ZIPLINE THROUGH A FOREST

From the Australian Outback to China's Nujiang Valley, for centuries ziplines have moved people, food, tools, and ammunition between peaks and over rivers. Modern fun seekers can choose from several courses near Portland. The two-hour Pumpkin Ridge Zip Tour eases people into the experience. The first of seven zip lines is fifteen feet off the ground, and then lines get faster, longer, and higher until people are soaring at a height of 120 feet. Skamania Lodge Adventures has a seven-line course plus an aerial park it describes as "*Swiss Family Robinson* meets *American Ninja*." Harnessed visitors leap between wobbly platforms in the trees. The Tree to Tree Adventure Park in Gaston, thirty miles west of Portland, includes a 1,280-foot super zip line, a tandem zip for racing a friend, and a sixty-five-foot platform you can jump off. Even if the additional aerial challenges seem too adrenaline provoking, the basic experience of ziplining through the treetops gives nature lovers an awe-inspiring new way to appreciate Oregon's Douglas fir forests.

Pumpkin Ridge Zip Tour:
71-371-3895
pumpkinridgeziptour.com

Skamania Lodge Zip Line Tour
509-427-0202
zipnskamania.com

Tree to Tree Adventure Park
503-357-0109
tree2treeadventurepark.com

WHEN TO GO: Spring to fall

HOURS: Varies

KID-FRIENDLY: Yes. Minimum age varies between courses but is usually around 7.

DOG-FRIENDLY: No

WHEELCHAIR ACCESSIBLE: No

EQUIPMENT NEEDED: A harness and helmet will be provided.

COST: Prices vary by course. Expect to spend approximately $85 per person for a zip course.

ACCESSIBLE BY PUBLIC TRANSPORTATION: No

DISTANCE FROM DOWNTOWN PORTLAND: Skamania Lodge, forty-five miles; Pumpkin Ridge, twenty-seven miles; Tree to Tree Adventure Park, thirty-three miles

FACILITIES: Varies

SPECIAL COMMENTS: Check the park's weight restrictions before you go. Some parks may insist on weighing you to be sure you qualify.

TOURS
360-693-2939

PHOTO CREDITS

1. Take a Kayaking Lesson—photo by Teresa Bergen

2. Float Down the Willamette River—photo by Teresa Bergen

3. Take the Polar Plunge—photo courtesy of Special Olympics Oregon

4. Raft the Clackamas River—photo courtesy of Blue Sky Rafting

5. Cruise on the *Portland Spirit*—photo courtesy of Portland Spirit

6. See Willamette Falls by Kayak—photo by Teresa Bergen

7. Play in a Fountain—photo by Teresa Bergen

8. Swim at Poet's Beach—photo by Teresa Bergen

9. Rent a Pedal Boat and Swim at Blue Lake Regional Park—photo by Teresa Bergen

10. Soak in Bagby Hot Springs—photo by Teresa Bergen

11. Experience the Waters of Belknap Hot Springs—photo by Teresa Bergen

12. Learn Stand-Up Paddleboarding Basics—photo courtesy of Alder Creek Kayak and Canoe

13. Try SUP Yoga—photo by Lauren Fields

14. Go Kayaking at Sunset—photo by Teresa Bergen

15. Explore a Waterfall—photo by Teresa Bergen

16. Careen Down the River on a Willamette Jetboat—photo courtesy of Willamette Jetboats

17. Go to the Beach at Sauvie Island—photo by Stu Mullenberg

18. Swim in an Outdoor Pool—photo courtesy of Portland Parks and Recreation, Portland, Oregon

19. Take a Luxury Cruise with UnCruise Adventures—photo by Teresa Bergen

20. Hike to Warrior Rock Lighthouse—photo by Teresa Bergen

21. Hike the Lower Macleay Park Trail—photo courtesy of the Forest Conservancy

22. Climb Council Crest—photo by Teresa Bergen

23. Unlock Biketown—photo courtesy of Biketown

24. Take a Segway Tour of Vancouver—photo by Teresa Bergen

25. Bike or Walk across Tilikum Crossing—photo by Teresa Bergen

26. Do the 4T Trail—photo by Teresa Bergen

27. Hike with the Mazamas—photo by Teresa Bergen

28. Explore Powell Butte Nature Park—photo by Teresa Bergen

29. Join a Pedalpalooza Event—photo by Ross Beach

30. Explore Oaks Bottom Wildlife Refuge—photo by Teresa Bergen

31. Cycle the Banks-Vernonia Trail—photo by Teresa Bergen

32. Pedal the Oregon Coast on Train Tracks—photo by Teresa Bergen

33. Run on a Track—photo by Teresa Bergen

34. Bike the Springwater Corridor—photo courtesy of Travel Portland

35. Participate in a $5 Fun Run—photo by Teresa Bergen

36. Go Cross-Country Skiing at Mount Hood—photo courtesy of Oregon's Mt. Hood Territory

37. Go Snowshoeing at Mount Hood—photo by Teresa Bergen

38. Tofurky Trot 5K—Photo courtesy of Northwest VEG

39. Starlight Run—photo courtesy of Starlight Run

40. Sunday Parkways—photo courtesy of Sunday Parkways

41. Tualatin Hills Nature Park—photo by Julia Demorest

42. Sauvie Island Birdwatching—photo by Teresa Bergen

43. Crystal Springs Rhododendron Garden—photo by Teresa Bergen

44. Hoyt Arboretum—photo courtesy of Hoyt Arboretum Friends

45. Audubon Sanctuary—by Amy Cave courtesy of the Audubon Society of Portland

46. Portland Japanese Garden—photo by Teresa Bergen

47. Count Fish on the Salmon Ladders at Bonneville Dam—photo by Teresa Bergen

48. Watch Swifts at Chapman School—photo by Teresa Bergen

49. Oregon Garden—photo by Teresa Bergen

50. Smith and Bybee Wetlands Natural Area—photo by Teresa Bergen

51. Peninsula Park Rose Garden—photo by Teresa Bergen

52. Oregon Zoo—photo by Brock Parker courtesy of Oregon Zoo

53. International Rose Test Garden—photo by Teresa Bergen

54. Leach Botanical Garden—photo by Teresa Bergen

55. Corgi Walk in the Pearl—photo by Teresa Bergen

56. First Caturday—photo by Teresa Bergen

57. Learn about Alpacas—photo by Heide Davis

58. Wooden Shoe Tulip Festival—photo by Teresa Bergen

59. The Grotto—photo by Teresa Bergen

60. Lan Su Chinese Garden—photo by Teresa Bergen

61. Heritage Trees—photo by Teresa Bergen

62. Goat Yoga—photo by Heather Davis

63. Forktown Food Tours—photo by Teresa Bergen

64. Original Practice Shakespeare Festival—photo by Teresa Bergen

65. Fort Vancouver National Historic Site—photo courtesy of Visit Vancouver USA

66. Japantown Walking Tour—photo by Teresa Bergen

67. Japanese American Historical Plaza—photo by Teresa Bergen

68. Portland Jewish Walking Tour—photo by Teresa Bergen

69. Apple Tasting Event—photo by Teresa Bergen

70. Get Spooked in Oregon City—photo by Teresa Bergen

71. Eat at Portland's Famous Food Carts—photo by Teresa Bergen

72. Urban Art Network First Thursday Art Walk—photo by Teresa Bergen

73. Last Thursday—photo by Rob Finch courtesy of Travel Portland

74. Tour Portland's Seedy Side—photo courtesy of Portland Walking Tours

75. Neighborhood Street Fairs—photo by Ross Beach

76. Saturday Market—photo by Jamie Francis courtesy of Travel Portland

77. Lone Fir Cemetery—photo by Teresa Bergen

78. Oregon Vietnam Veterans Memorial—photo by Teresa Bergen

79. Hawthorne Ghost Tours—photo by Teresa Bergen

80. Portland Highland Games—photo by Teresa Bergen

81. Movies in the Park—photo courtesy Portland Parks and Recreation, Portland, Oregon

82. Winter Light Festival—photo by Teresa Bergen

83. Rose Festival—photo by Teresa Bergen

84. Beverly Cleary Sculpture Garden—photo by Teresa Bergen

85. Enchanted Forest—photo by Teresa Bergen

86. Clark County Fair—photo courtesy of Visit Vancouver USA

87. Go Flightseeing with Envi Adventures—photo by Teresa Bergen

88. Oaks Park—photo by Teresa Bergen

89. Original Corn Maize on Sauvie Island—photo courtesy of the Maize at the Pumpkin Patch

90. West Coast Fitness' Outdoor Training Yard—photo by Teresa Bergen

91. Harper's Playground—photo by Teresa Bergen

92. Winter Wonderland at PDX Raceway—photo courtesy of Portland Police Bureau Sunshine Division

93. Zoo Lights—photo by Jamie Francis courtesy of Travel Portland

94. Take Fido to a Dog Park—photo by Teresa Bergen

95. Practice Your Swing at a Public Golf Course—photo courtesy of Portland Parks and Recreation, Portland, Oregon

96. Play Horseshoes in Laurelhurst Park—photo by Teresa Bergen

97. Geocaching—photo by Jamie Francis courtesy of Travel Portland

98. Cosmic Tubing at Mount Hood—photo courtesy of Oregon's Mt. Hood Territory

99. Portland Adult Soapbox Derby—photo by Teresa Bergen

100. Zipline through a Forest—photo courtesy of Skamania Lodge Adventures

INDEX